Barbecue and Outdoor Cookery

Barbecue and Outdoor Cookery

Barbara Logan

*Happy barbecuing! and
with all good wishes.*

Barbara.

December 1978.

WARD LOCK LIMITED·LONDON

© Barbara Logan 1978
First published in Great Britain in 1978
by Ward Lock Limited, 116 Baker Street,
London W1M 2BB, a member of the Pentos Group.

Text filmset in 11 on 12pt. 'Monophoto' Baskerville
by Servis Filmsetting Limited, Manchester
Printed and bound in Hong Kong by
Mandarin Publishers Ltd

British Library Cataloguing in Publication Data

Logan, Barbara
    Barbecue and outdoor cookery.
    1. Barbecue cookery
    I. Title
    641.5'78   TX840.B3

ISBN 07063 5714 0 P/BK.

Contents

Acknowledgements

The publishers and author would like to thank the following for their kindness and co-operation in supplying illustrations and recipes for this book.

Bacofoil Ltd. (p. 18)
British Sausage Bureau (p. 35)
Carmel Produce Information Bureau (p. 70)
New Zealand Lamb Information Bureau (jacket illustration; p. 87; p. 8?
Olives from Spain (p. 69)
and Lee and Perrins Schwartz Spices Skewer Bureau for supplying recip
R. & C. Vintners (p. 70)
Unigate Dairies (p. 36)
John West Ltd. (p. 17; p. 36)

Introduction

The popularity of eating out of doors has brought the barbecue into its own so that it is now accepted as an informal, fun way of cooking as well as entertaining.

It first appeared when man discovered how to kindle a fire and found out that his food tasted better cooked. The next great leap forward in cooking occurred when man invented the spit. The barbecue saw its halcyon days and indeed got its name, when it was commonplace for people to celebrate by roasting a whole beast – '*de barbe à queue*' (from beard to tail) on a spit, usually on the village green in Europe or in the cattle- and sheep-grazing prairies and pampas of far-off lands.

Today barbecuing has developed into the art of cooking somewhat smaller morsels of meat and vegetables in a much more sophisticated way and with more succulent results. Nevertheless, the barbecue itself remains essentially a very simple means of cooking and can easily be improvized almost anywhere.

For example, you set up a grate between bricks with the fire made on a sheet of foil below it in your garden; at the beach by burning readily available drift-wood or, in the country, by digging a small pit while others in the party collect firewood. If a grate is not available wire mesh or expanded metal can be used instead. Some people become so adept at this level that they just build a slightly more elaborate cooking range in their garden and, with no further frills or gadgetry, seem able to produce all manner of dishes in whatever quantity is required and – the most outstanding accomplishment of the outdoor chef – at the right time.

Few of us are endowed with such gifts. The rest need to be helped, and perhaps the main reason why barbecuing has become so popular is that all manner of aids and gadgets have been developed to help almost anyone become a master barbecue chef. One has only to look at the displays of barbecuing equipment and accessories at garden centres and department stores to appreciate how well the barbecuing enthusiast is catered for and what an attractive, practical and sometimes sophisticated cooking appliance the barbecue has become.

A closer look at these displays will disclose a wide variety of types and models of barbecue so it immediately becomes apparent that it is not as easy as one might think to choose the right one. While some people might be satisfied with a simple brazier, others may only be content with the latest innovations, such as electrically operated revolving spits. It is not unusual for some barbecues to incorporate a small oven (complete with thermometer), a hood (to keep the smoke in) or a windshield (to control the draught and smoke), a fan or bellows to help kindle the fire and a poker to stir the embers.

The colour and temperature of these embers will become the focus of attention of the would-be barbecuer, who will need to become familiar with the various barbecue briquets now on the market. Some people prefer these to plain charcoal, according to the claims which are variously made as to how quickly they light or how slowly or hot they burn. The choice of fire lighters is most important. Petrol or kerosene should *never* be used because they are dangerous and give the food an unpleasant taste. Some woods can be used which release attractive aromas as they burn (though hardwood briquets are the most widely recommended) and if the fire should be smokeless – which under certain conditions is desirable, if not always attainable by the beginner – then there are sauces which can give the food that possibly missing smoky taste!

Nevertheless, in spite of all these aids, barbecuing is still not an exact science. There are so many uncertainties: fires that will not start, that burn too hot, may cook too fast. The greatest uncertainty stems from the fact that it is usually Dad who does the barbecuing and, until he has established some sort of reputation, his family and his guests may well wonder what sort of a barbecued meal they are going to get!

In this book we hope to reduce all these uncertainties by helping the would-be barbecuer to choose the equipment best suited to his needs, advising him on how to operate it, and providing him with a selection of recipes. Armed with these he should be able to spit roast and grill every kind of meat, poultry, game and fish – and indeed, vegetables and fruit too. There will also be described a variety of ways of preparing food for the barbecue including marinating, devilling and tenderizing, and the secrets will be disclosed about how to make a wide selection of sauces and dressings to baste the food with whilst it is cooking and to serve with it.

Furthermore, as the barbecue is a truly international form of cooking, recipes will be drawn from many countries where cooking on a spit or brazier is traditional, like the Middle and Far East.

In some countries, like China and Japan, the barbecue has actually been brought indoors. The secret lies in making a smokeless fire and ensuring adequate ventilation, so there is no reason why, even in deepest winter, a trial 'cook-out' should not be held in, say, the garage for a start; as soon as the fire is under control and giving off no smoke it can be brought indoors and put in the fire-place (see below for further information). In this way the barbecue can be used all the year round, regardless of the vagaries of the weather, and the barbecuer will be able to consider himself an all-rounder in this gentle art.

CHOOSING A BARBECUE

If you have never used a barbecue before, the best advice is to borrow one or to improvize along the lines of the more elementary types described on page 22 and so gain practical experience of kindling the fire and cooking on it. Alternatively, a small cheap barbecue can be bought which will always come in handy later on for keeping food warm. The hints on pages 12 and 13 should then be followed.

Another good way of getting experience is to help at other people's barbecue parties. Some hosts will let their guests cook their own steaks, for instance, and with a little encouragement the experienced barbecue chef might be persuaded to pass on some of his secrets, for barbecuing is inclined to be a highly individual art.

Assuming, then, that our beginner has had an initiation into barbecuing without necessarily undergoing a veritable 'trial by fire', and acquiring on the way some idea as to what he wants and how many he wants to cater for, he should select one of the following basic alternatives and so will immediately reduce the scope of his search. If, for instance, he does not care for a portable barbecue as he has a suitable site to build one in his garden he may prefer a permanent fixture.

If, however, he wants something portable, then he must decide whether he prefers the kind he can use indoors as well as outdoors. As ventilation is the main problem indoors (charcoal, it must be remembered, gives off carbon monoxide fumes which are poisonous) the chimney breast must be large enough to collect and draw up all the smoke and fumes into the chimney. The indoor unit must be so designed that it fits over the grate of the fire-place, leaving enough room for the forward or outward movement of the grill and fire-pan of the barbecue for easy access to tend to the food and the fuel. This choice will therefore be restricted to those units which will fit into the particular fire-place and should be chosen carefully and, preferably, with professional advice. However, any brazier or Hibachi-type of barbecue of the right size should be suitable as long as it fits and, exercising the two options, is well worth a try as the opportunities for barbecuing are enormously increased. On the other hand, if 'indoors' means the garage or a shelter in which to take cover in bad weather, then any of the portable barbecues described in the following pages will be suitable. Portable barbecues include, of course, those which are collapsible or can be carried by hand as well as on wheels.

The remaining choice for the beginner is now between the two types of brazier barbecue most commonly in use today.

THE TRADITIONAL HIBACHI (literally 'fire box')

This has hardly changed over the centuries and consists of a cast iron (or

The Anatomy of the
Hibachi Brazier

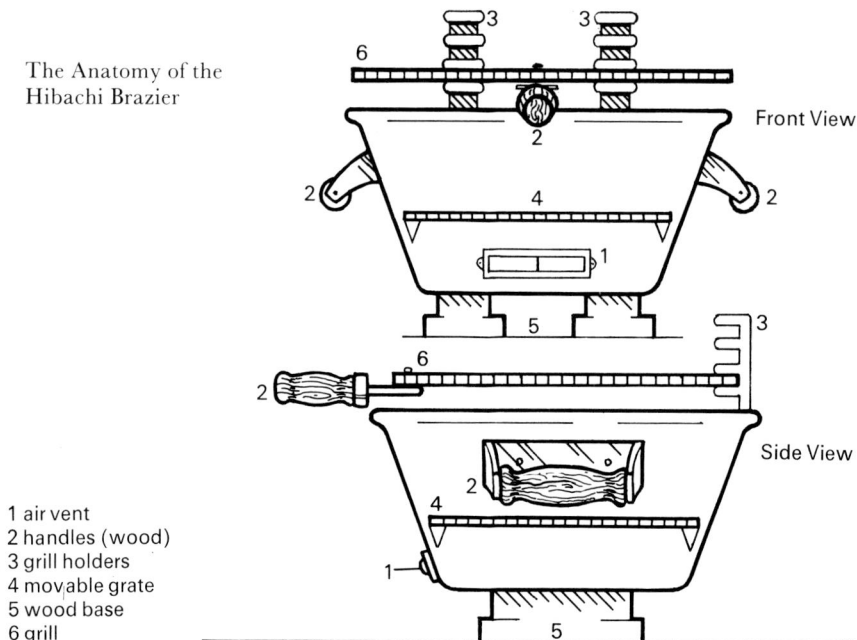

Front View

Side View

1 air vent
2 handles (wood)
3 grill holders
4 movable grate
5 wood base
6 grill

cast aluminium) fire box with a removable fire grate, a draught control vent near the base and a cast iron (or aluminium) grill for which there are usually three or four cooking levels to raise the food above the fire. They can be round or rectangular and are now also available in a variety of colours. (See 'The Anatomy of the Hibachi' on page 10.)

While the cooking area of a single Hibachi is small (only big enough to cook for four people) Hibachis are also available in double and triple table-top units on small wooden bases. Free-standing models are also available on legs and on wheels. All the handles for the grate and for carrying the units are usually made of wood so that the braziers can be easily moved from place to place, whether in use or not. The draught control vent is a great help in lighting the fire and afterwards in controlling the heat and for removing cinders and ash. It should be noted that Hibachis carry a manufacturer's warning against using

Free standing Hibachi braziers

Single, double and triple Hibachi braziers

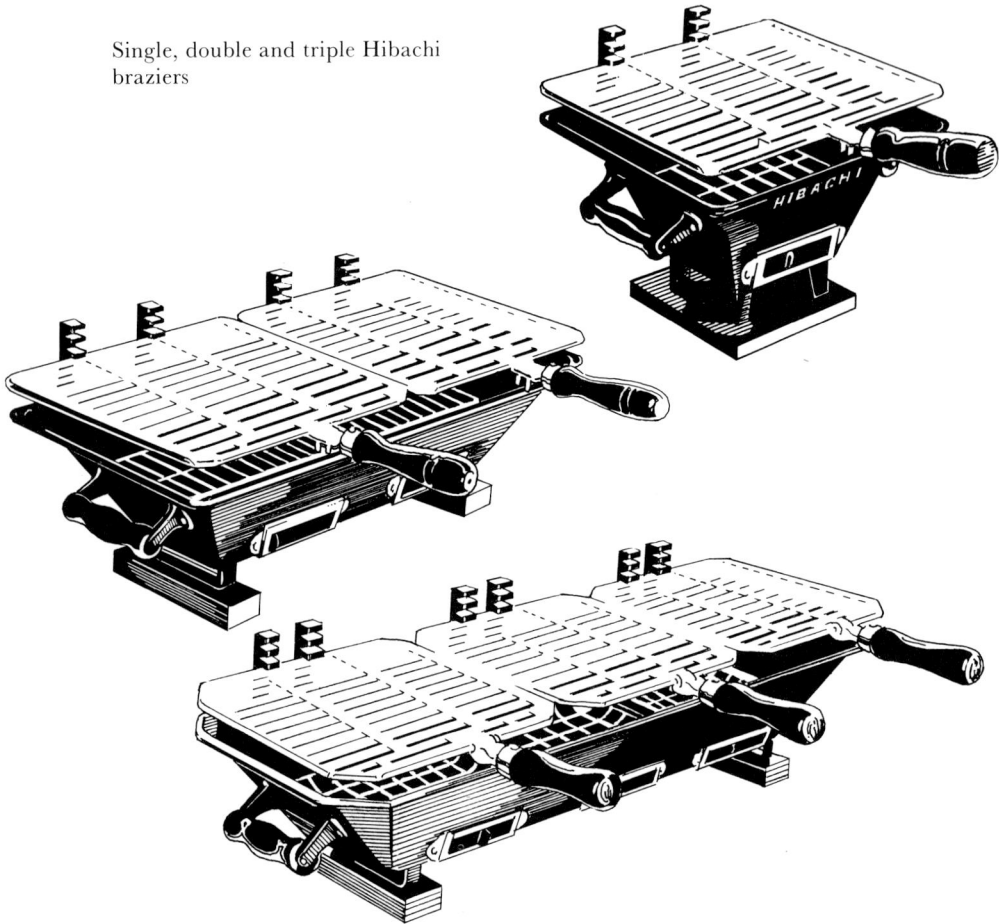

them indoors or in confined spaces. Most Hibachis are designed along classical lines and are sturdily built. Altogether, they are simple, efficient and usually inexpensive braziers. (See 'Models' above.)

THE BARBECUE GRILL BRAZIER (sometimes referred to as the standard barbecue)

This consists, in its simplest form, of a bowl made of heavy gauge sheet metal to hold the fire and a usually adjustable, revolving wire grill above it. (See 'The Evolution of the Barbecue Brazier on page 14.) The most important points to examine before buying this type of barbecue are the thickness and quality of the metal used for the fire bowl (usually treated with a heat-resistant finish) and of the wire used to make the grill. While the former should be tough enough to stand up to great heat for long periods, additional protection and longer life can be given by laying gravel and foil on the fire bowl but the grill should be made of chrome or nickel-plated stout steel wire to withstand the direct heat of the fire below. The wires of the grill should be close enough to prevent small pieces of food, such as sausages, from falling through into the fire.

Only braziers with adjustable grills are recommended, so that the grill can be raised through a central pivot or by moving it up or down a set of at least three grill-holders fixed along the circumference of the bowl of the barbecue. Any other way of varying the cooking temperature, such as tilting the grill or revolving it to put the food over a cooler or hotter part of the fire-bowl is not entirely satisfactory, except for those usually larger models where the fire-pan itself can be moved up and down.

The simple type of brazier described above is generally available from about 30cm/12in in diameter on short or collapsible legs for picnics and up to about 60cm/24in in diameter in free-standing models. The rectangular picnic version starts at around 24cm/10in by 37.5cm/15in and is also usually collapsible; while the full-size free-standing model is about twice as big, often having two grills about 25cm/10in by 37.5cm/15in each.

It should be noted though that free-standing barbecues do tend to be or to become rather unstable, and there is nothing quite as infuriating as trying to cook and manage the fire on a wobbly barbecue. In the best designs the legs are usually braced on to a shelf below the barbecue on which food and plates can be stacked. Their combined weight acts as ballast and improves stability. The problem becomes particularly acute in the larger barbecues because of the high superstructure, and yet some have only three legs and two are likely to be on wheels. These, incidentally, should be made of metal with solid rubber tyres—plastic wheels are sometimes fitted which may be firm when new but have a tendency to become soft and cause wobbling in a relatively short time. The wisdom of looking carefully into the stability of free-standing barbecues will become even more apparent as we examine the superstructure of some of the larger models. (See 'Wagon Barbecues' on page 20.)

The advent of *the spit* – or rotisserie – as a built-in accessory of the

The Evolution of the Barbecue Brazier

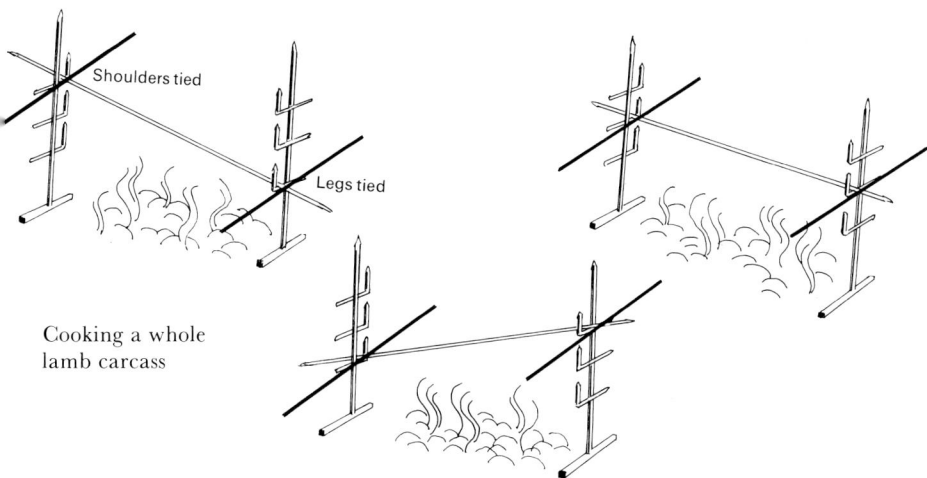

Shoulders tied

Legs tied

Cooking a whole
lamb carcass

barbecue is probably the greatest single development in outdoor cooking since the brazier barbecue itself became so popular. With this the barbecue became a sophisticated cooking appliance. Whether the spit was first attached to a wind-shield around the brazier (a useful addition in its own right), or *vice versa*, it has seemed natural enough that the wind-shield should have developed a hood and that on many models both have combined to become an oven, or at least a place in which food and plates can be kept warm. The appearance of a battery-powered motor to revolve the spit seems to have been just as timely as the advent of aluminium foil for laying the fire and wrapping the food!

When selecting a barbecue with a spit, the most important features to check are the steadiness of the whole apparatus and the quality of the spit and its accessories. As a simple test, when examining one of these barbecues on display just tot up the approximate weight of the bri-quets, the fire-base, the food, plates and possibly some cooked food on an upper warming grill – probably not far short of 7kilos/15lbs – quite enough to make any but the most sturdy barbecues wobble! One way to counteract this is to put about the same weight in food, coals, plates and accessories on the shelf below the barbecue.

The spit should have three or four pairs of supports on each side of the brazier so that it can be raised, lowered *and* tilted. It should be suitably thick for its overall length and should have a wooden handle at one end and enough to spare at the other to fit a motor if one is not built in. Two sturdy forks or tines to hold the meat on the spit should be secured to it by thumb-screws – though they will be so hot by the time the meat is cooked, or needs to be adjusted, that a pair of pliers will come in very

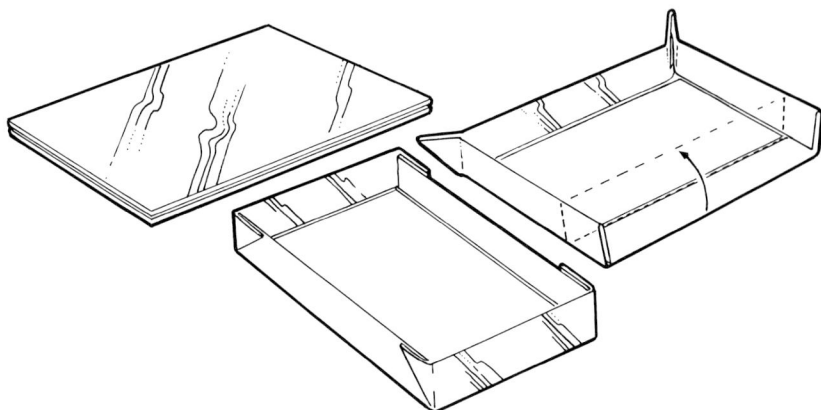

handy. There are various other accessories for the spit (see page 28) some of which, like the drip pan, can be made of foil. (See illustration above.)

The remaining portable barbecues which are worth considering are all large and hardly likely to become the beginner's choice. They are nevertheless of general interest and even beginners will no doubt want to know something about the way they function and the features which make them different from the others we have discussed.

WAGON BARBECUES

These have been referred to briefly on page 13. (See illustrations on page 20.) Apart from their larger size they mainly differ from the hooded grills in two respects. First the hood has a hinged extension over the front so that the spit is completely enclosed, thus providing an oven-like space for warming plates and food; and second the fire-pan itself can be raised and lowered within the fire-box in order to regulate the amount of heat reaching the grill or the spit. This is very useful, especially if the spit is being used, as the fire can be pushed slightly towards the rear of the fire-box leaving room in front of the fire for a drip pan directly below the spit. These barbecues cater for as many as two dozen people if the menu is not too extensive. They have generous working areas on either side of the hood and a shelf below on which sturdy legs are braced, and on at least one pair of which there are somewhat larger 'wagon' wheels.

Mandarin chicken bundles (p. 72)

Barbecue cooking with foil see pages 27–28

KETTLE GRILLS

These are mostly free-standing, covered, round (40cm/16in to 55cm/ 22in) or oval (at most about 60cm/24in wide) braziers made of cast aluminium or steel plate, stainless or enamelled. (See illustration on page 21.) The top half is usually hinged to the lower but is capable of standing upright, and in that position also acts as a windshield. The bottom half is the fire bowl and is very deep to accommodate the fire on a grate below the grill, and a removable ash pan below the grate also acts as a vent. Generally, either the grill or the grate can be raised or lowered through two or three positions. There is another vent at the top of the lid and the fire is controlled by adjusting these two vents which can be closed to put out the fire. The results obtained from cooking on this type of barbecue are very similar to those obtained in an oven except for the effect of the embers and the smoke which the fire makes. The kettle grill is ideal in windy weather, but its greatest virtue must be for the chef who knows exactly how to control the fire and so can tell quite accurately when the food is cooked without having to lift the lid too often. It is ideal for the preparation of a single dish, such as a large joint or fish with all the trimmings, for a set of number of persons who, the chef hopes, will all sit down to the meal at the same time.

There are many other types of barbecues but we shall mention only two more which are usually available in the shops: the fully *electric* and the fully *gas* operated barbecues. We say 'fully' because there are electric or gas fire starters, but we are referring to those barbecues which can be plugged into the electricity mains or into a container of bottled gas which can conveniently be carried on the barbecue (see page 21). In both cases either a ceramic substance or pieces of lava rock take the place of charcoal and briquets and become red hot and cook in the same way – by radiating heat on to the food on the grill or spit above. The great advantage here is that it can be set at precisely the degree of heat desired. Neither makes smoke but can be used to smoke food by placing chips of dampened hickory or fruit wood on to the heated 'briquets' and by closing the hood. They can be used indoors with normal ventilation.

SMOKE COOKING (and *not* **Smoking** or **Smoke Curing**)

These are quite distinct, although in the Chinese smoke oven, where the meat cooks in a chimney well away from the coals, the two do approach

Wagon barbecues

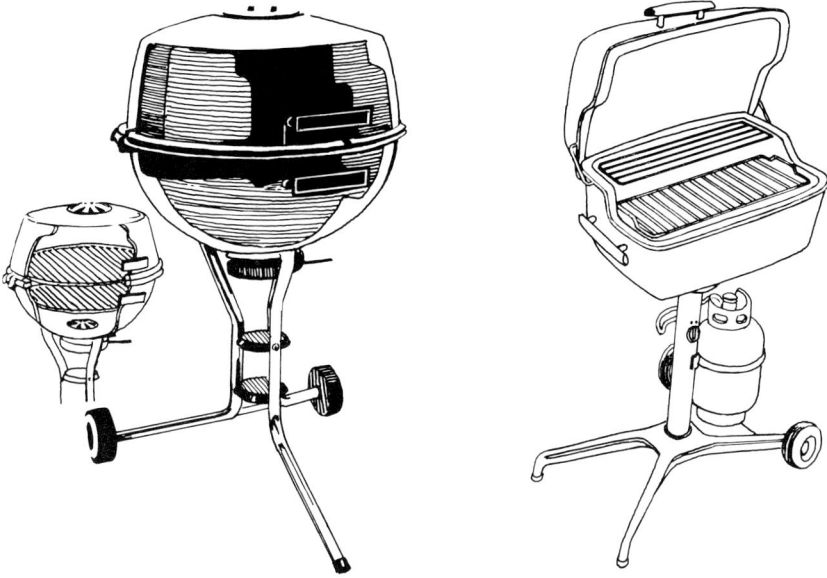

Kettle grills

each other. In smoke cooking, the heat cooks the food and the smoke imparts the flavour. This can be done in a covered barbecue and takes about the same time as oven cooking the same foods. Smoking is more of a curing process than a cooking process in that the smoke causes certain chemical changes in the meat which render it edible. Furthermore, true smoking takes days and uses little heat. Smoke cooking is often done on cold or windy days because the cover enables an even temperature to be maintained above the fire. To strengthen the smoke flavour any of the following can be added: chips or twigs of aromatic wood, small quantities of damp sawdust (but not of pine or other resinous woods), hickory chips, garlic, thyme, rosemary or bay leaves.

Do-it-yourself barbecues

Having considered all types of barbecues which people might wish to buy, we feel some consideration must be given to those who prefer to improvize whenever the urge takes them to barbecue, and at the other extreme, those who know so precisely what they want that they build a do-it-yourself barbecue in the garden.

So first to the improvizers – such as the fisherman who gets a sudden urge to cook his catch. All too often around lakes and rivers people dump all sorts of containers, tins and flower pots, and where the fishing is good it is quite likely someone will have had an old bucket for bait and then have left it behind. An old bucket makes an ideal barbecue and if it has a hole in the side to serve as an air vent so much the better. A bucket can in fact make such a good barbecue that there are braziers on the market which are effectively buckets with an air vent on the side and a grill over the top. (See illustration opposite.) So all our fisherman has to do is to find something he can use as a grill, such as pieces of wire woven together, bits of expanded metal or, better still and more easily found, a piece of chicken wire.

However, in the absence of a bucket or anything better, a few bricks arranged in two rows with something to act as a grill between then will do just as well (See illustrations opposite.)

When it comes to searching for fuel, people are best off at the beach where there is usually plenty of driftwood. Elsewhere, they may have to look further afield, but bits of firewood can be come by, and paper, cardboard and dry leaves can help to kindle the fire. People who try this and find it enjoyable often become addicted to picnic barbecuing and then take a portable barbecue or at least the bare essentials to make one. Disposable barbecues are also available. (See illustration opposite.)

For those who hanker after a taste of the medieval way of life there are two ways of cooking the whole carcass of a lamb which only require do-it-yourself techniques.

a)

b)

c)

d)

e)

f)

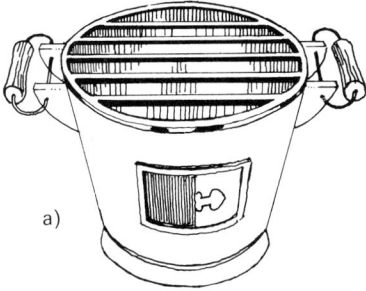

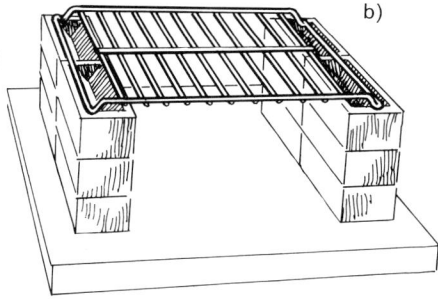

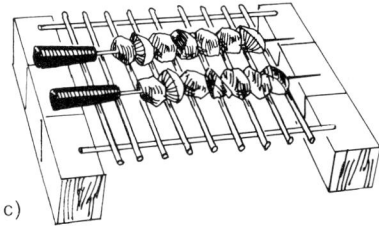

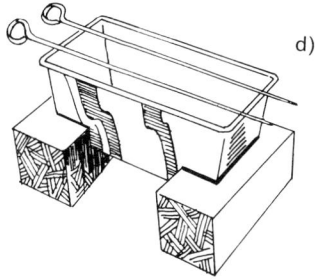

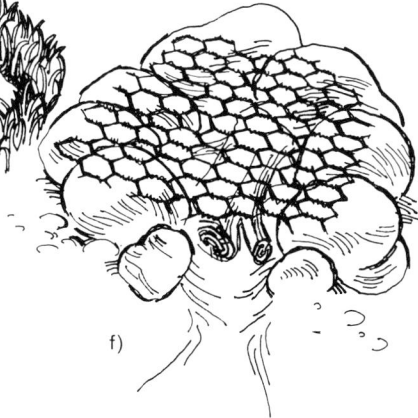

Simple brazier barbecues

One is a New Zealand way of holding a celebration – by cooking a lamb carcass – called a Hangi. They dig a pit and lay a lamb carcass over glowing coals mixed with large stones, then cover it completely with leaves. Twenty four hours later, the lamb is cooked to perfection and the festivities begin!

The other method is also for cooking a whole lamb but this time on a spit. The equipment required is as follows:

A double cruciform spit resting on two uprights in three positions, level, tilted one way or tilted the opposite way (see diagram on page 15)

1 10 kilo/20lb bag of charcoal

12 bricks to form surround to fire

Foil for base of fire

1 large box of fire lighters

String

Trussing needle

When preparing the fire ensure that the ground is adequately protected. Place foil to form a base for the fire and use the bricks to form a surround. Charcoal and fire lighters can then be placed inside. Ignite the fire approximately half an hour before placing the lamb on to cook, so that adequate time is allowed for the charcoal to become hot and for excess smoke to burn off.

Half split the lamb down the backbone, and lie a New Zealand lamb carcass flat on the cruciform. Position the lamb carcass on the cruciform spit so that the inside of the lamb is flat down on the central bar. Tie both legs and shoulders securely to the metal cross bars. Then secure the backbone to the central bar using a trussing needle and string.

Sprinkle the carcass with salt. Place the cruciform spit in slots on the stand so that the shoulders are at the nearest level to the fire. Alternate the position of the carcass throughout the cooking time, (approximately every $\frac{1}{2}$ hour), so that the legs are at the nearer level to the fire and, by turning the carcass over, so that the skin is exposed to the heat. Total cooking time is approximately 5 hours, but test as you go.

Building a permanent barbecue by do-it-yourself methods requires sufficient care to ensure that it will not turn out to be a folly, an eye-sore, or a source of discomfort to owner and neighbours alike. There are, of course, ways of avoiding this, especially if a sheltered situation can be found in the garden which fulfills all the desirable, practical and aesthetic considerations. It is safest however, to have a trial run with a simple temporary barbecue made with a few bricks and a grill. A

24

common secondary stage is a conversion from an existing incinerator and this is not likely to raise problems beyond the actual design so that the resulting installation serves both purposes adequately.

The more advanced stage is likely to include do-it-yourself enthusiasts who are expert enough to design and construct however large a permanent barbecue they may require. They may find the design above interesting.

We give below details of the sort of barbecue which almost anyone could build or adapt to make their own design. Attachments recommended above for portable barbecues can also be adapted, but however permanent the structure is, these attachments should always be

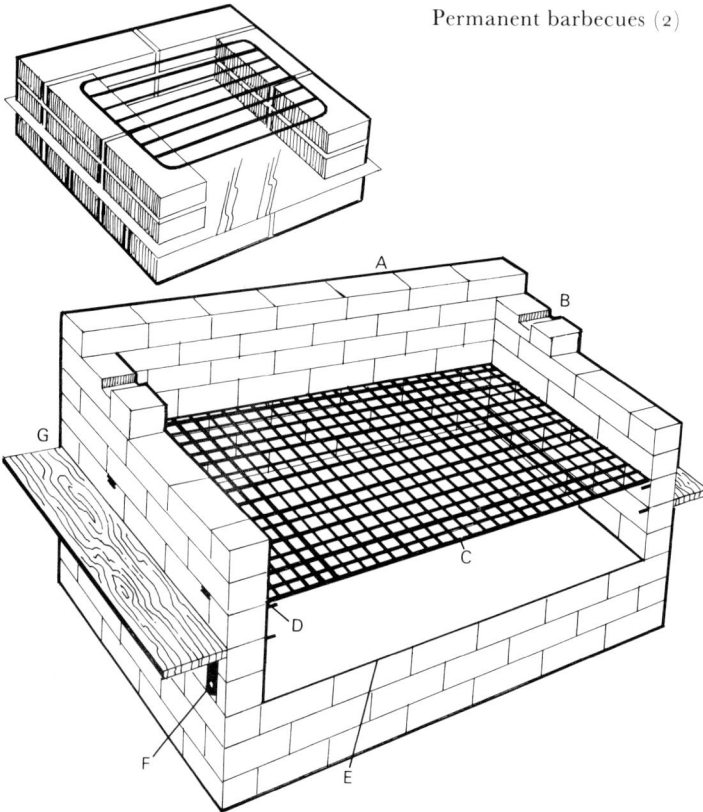

easily removable for storage. The following details relate to the diagram above.

A Firebricks are ideal but ordinary bricks are adequate.

B Grooves to hold spit/rotisserie may be incorporated.

C Grills should not have gaps larger than 1 sq. cm/$\frac{1}{2}$sq. in or food may fall through.

D Grill should be 15–38cm/6–14in above the top of the charcoal. Metal brackets built into the barbecue, with convenient spacing, allow you to move the grill up and down.

E A gravel base helps ventilation although ordinary brick is adequate.

F Brackets, either built into the original construction or subsequently bolted on, to support the work surface.

G Wooden shelf, suitable for preparing food or laying out utensils ready to use.

26

Accessories for the barbecue

Most people like to buy gadgets and kitchen aids and there are lots which can be bought to go with a barbecue. No doubt after a time some will be discarded, but a few items will remain as old faithfuls and come out every time you barbecue. (See illustrations on pages 30–31.)

Cooking gloves are a 'must', either cotton padded gloves or asbestos oven-mitts.

An apron to protect you from grease splashes during the cooking and cinders.

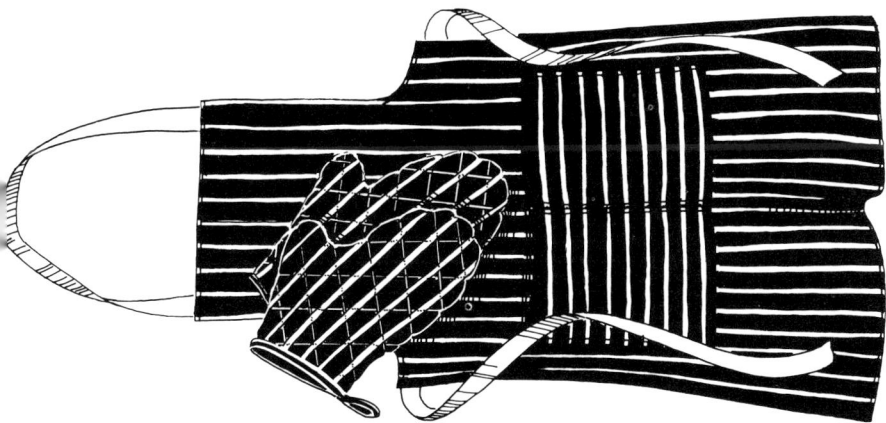

Foil: This is possibly the most versatile aid.

For the barbecue: to lay (shiny side up) a protective foundation between the fire-box and the fire; to make drip pans, to improvize a baking tray, to use as heat reflector, (shiny-side downwards), by making a hood over the barbecue or simply by laying a sheet above and/or beside the spit and in innumerable other ways.

For the food: to wrap it up before and during cooking and, after the food is cooked, to keep it warm. In addition there are many items which can be moulded in foil to cook the food in, especially when camping, or to replace a forgotten or broken utensil. (See diagram page 29.)

At least two *sharp knives*, one medium sized and one larger are handy to have near the barbecue.

Two *tongs* are needed, both with long handles; one for stoking the fire and arranging the coals in it and another for placing small pieces of meat, sausages, etc. to cook on the fire and to move them around on the grill. A pair of shorter tongs can also be useful for heavier pieces of meat or fish. Some have one side shaped like a spatula for turning over the food.

The cooking tongs are usually part of a set which should include the following, all long and wooden-handled;

a spatula for cooking and serving

a fork

a spoon

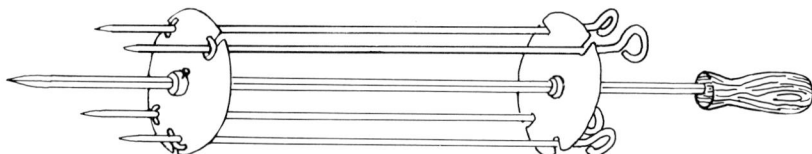

Accessories for
the spit

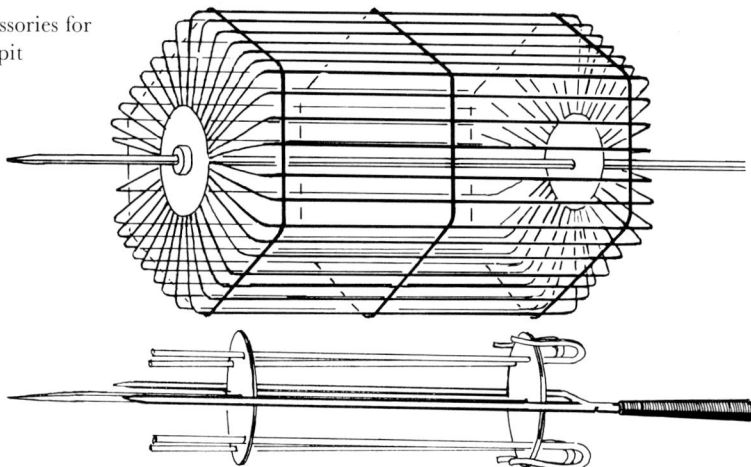

Some uses of foil

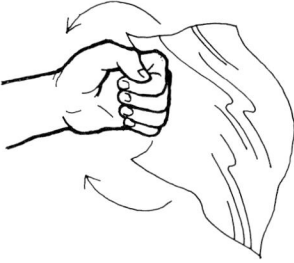

replacement
container

grill hood

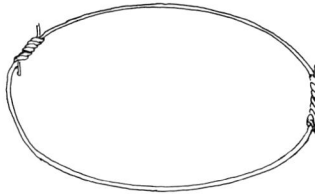

as many basting brushes as may be needed according to the variety of
bastes and sauces which are going to be applied to the food. These
brushes should be made of pure bristle – nylon and plastic bristles are
inclined to fall prey to the fire

A stiff metal brush is very useful for keeping the grill clean.

Hinged wire baskets These are called hinged grills if the wire is thick
enough for them to be used as a grill. There are square and round ones
and they are most useful for cooking hamburgers and fish, or small
pieces of chicken or sausages.

Some useful accessories

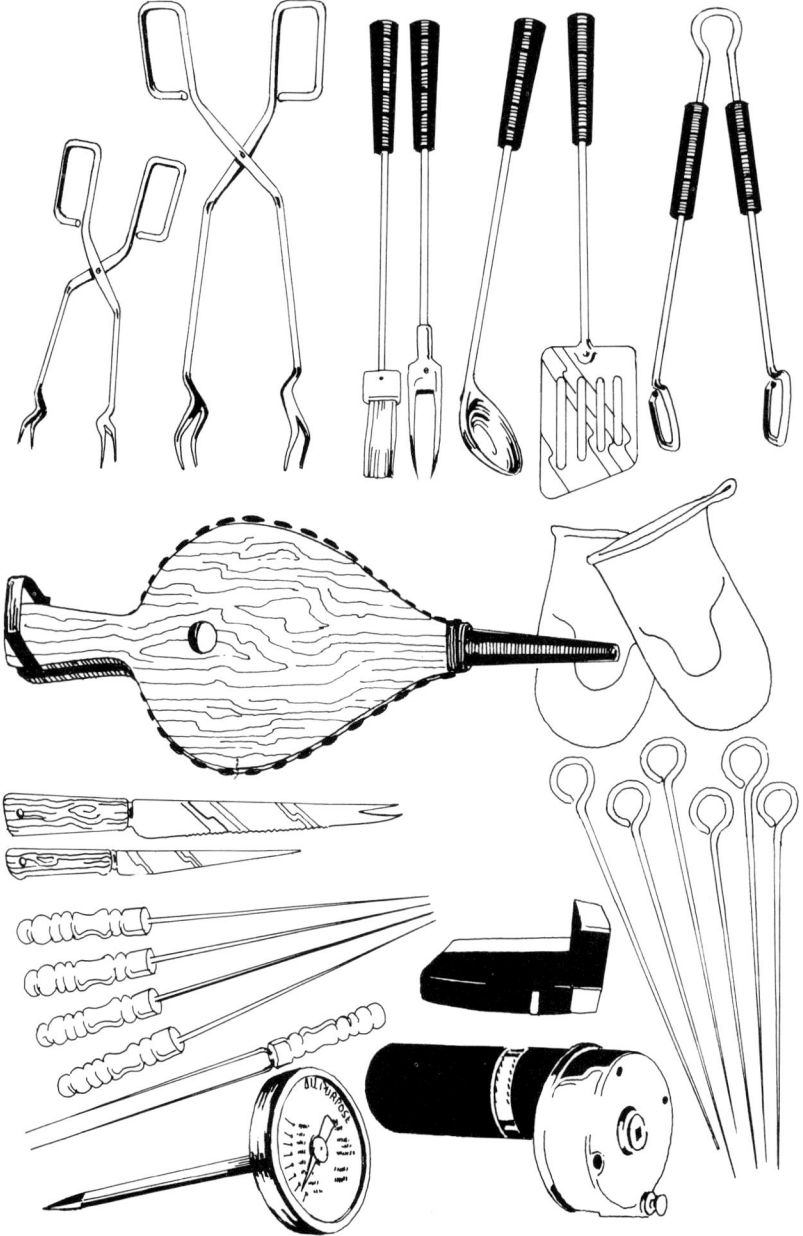

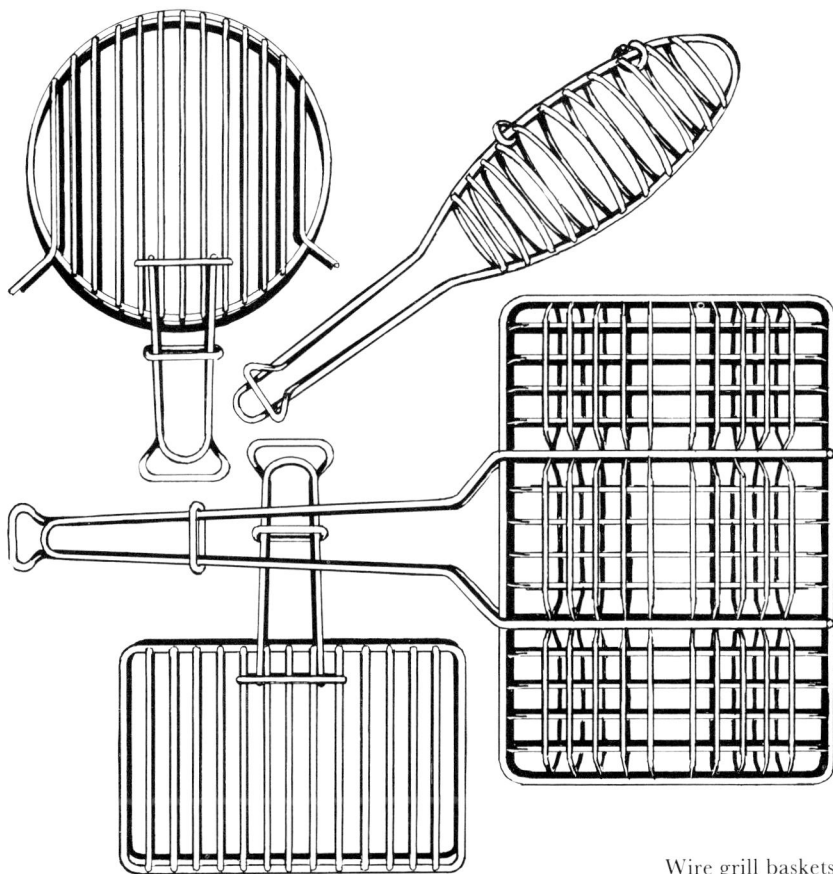

Wire grill baskets

Metal skewers (preferably stainless steel) should be as long as possible so that the grip does not go over the coals. Wooden handles are recommended. Or you can improvize with long metal knitting needles.

A battery-operated spit motor is a necessary accessory if not supplied with the barbecue and balancing weights make its task somewhat lighter; they enable you to get the spit to revolve evenly by equalizing the weights around it.

Extra forks (or tines) and short skewers are worth having – there are also four-pronged forks which can get a better hold on a piece of meat or poultry.

Two other imaginative attachments give the spit two entirely different extra uses. One is for cooking kebabs and the other for cooking small pieces of meat, vegetables or even fruit, such as pineapple chunks. To use these attachments remove the forks from the spit and thread on to the spit the kebab holder or the basket. (See diagrams p 28.)

Additional check list
    Carving board
    Large salt and pepper shakers
    Sprinkler – small watering can or squirter to douse unwanted flames
    Meat thermometer
    Bellows – in case the fire should need a little encouragement
    Kitchen roll – indispensable for so many odd jobs from mopping up to serviettes
    First aid kit

The fire

FUELS

Hardwood charcoal briquets are recommended for good cooking results. They burn longer than lump charcoal and give out more heat. They are made from dense hardwoods with a low resin content – usually beech, oak or birch. Briquets are uniform in size and so are easier to arrange in the fire box. They are packed in 3, 5 and 10 kilos/6, 10, and 20lbs bags and are obtainable from garden centres, supermarkets, hardware stores and, sometimes, at petrol stations. Light the fire 30–45 minutes before starting to cook.

Lumpwood charcoal is usually made from softwood as well as hardwood and this mixture will often give off sparks. It is the softwood which has a high resin content and can flavour the food. Again, lump charcoal, as its name implies comes in lumps of varying sizes which are not easy to arrange unless the larger pieces are broken up, and while it ignites rather more easily than most untreated briquets, it also burns faster and so requires rather more frequent attention. Light the fire 20–30 minutes before starting to cook.

Specially treated charcoal briquets can be obtained that ignite readily. They do not produce flames and, in fact, unless the draught is very strong, they do not glow red in the day-time, but a fine grey ash is produced on the surface of each briquet as the fire spreads.

It must be remembered that burning charcoal fumes contain carbon monoxide which is highly poisonous, so when cooking indoors be sure the room is well ventilated and place the barbecue over the grate in the fireplace so that the chimney can draw up the fumes.

FIRE LIGHTERS

Where there is fire danger lurks, so it is quite unnecessary to increase the risk by using petrol, naphtha, Kerosene and lighter fluid. Besides, they all give the food an unpleasant taste.

Better use self-igniting charcoal, the well-known solid white block fire lighter, which is also available in granulated form, methylated spirits or jellied alcohol. There are other liquid fire lighters on the market but do check what they are made of. Gas torches (or blow-lamps) and electric fire lighters are unquestionably the neatest, cleanest, most efficient and least dangerous.

Nevertheless, some people still prefer to kindle fires and there is no doubt that kindling a fire generates a rather delightful sensation of suspense and expectancy, especially among the more hungry members of the party.

LIGHTING THE FIRE

There is no reason why anyone should find it difficult to light a fire if they follow these instructions carefully.

1 Cover the base of the barbecue completely with heavy-duty foil or a double thickness of the standard foil, shiny side up. If you want to lay a fire-base of dry gravel, vermiculite or asbestos (only really necessary for frequent barbecuing or if the bottom of the barbecue is suspect) then place another sheet of foil over it, but this time make small perforations in it with a fork to allow the air to come through to the fire and the fat and grease to seep through into the fire-base, leaving the coals and cinders above so that they can be gathered and conveniently removed after the barbecue is over, and then sifted from the ash and kept for the next time.

2 Place on the foil whichever you have or prefer of the following: (a) twisted paper and kindling wood chips; or (b)
a few small pieces of white solid fire-lighter (or a handful of the granules) and a few small pieces of charcoal or broken-up briquets; or (c)
small pieces of charcoal and/or briquets and methylated spirits.

3 Then put six to eight briquets or larger pieces of charcoal above and around whichever you have chosen from this list and set light to it.
   There are a few refinements and combinations to this list such as pouring some methylated spirits over the kindling wood in (a); by marinating the kindling wood, the pieces of charcoal or the briquets in methylated spirits in (a), (b), or (c); using a torch or blow-lamp on either of the three; replacing the fire-lighters and kindling wood by a pack of self-igniting charcoal.

4 Sometimes though a fire simply will not start. This is more likely to

34

Barbecued sausages with sweet and sour sauce (pp. 49 and 56)

Peach and grape tartlets (p. 98), grapefruit mould (p. 98) orange cheesecake (p. 99)
Refreshing desserts for a summer barbecue

occur with braziers which have no built-in draught control or vent, so a draught can only be induced by fanning or using bellows. In this situation it is often recommended to employ what is called in barbecuing circles a 'chimney'. It is, in fact, just a large juice or coffee can from which both top and bottom have been removed and air holes made round one end which becomes the base of the chimney. Stand the chimney on the grate of the brazier, place the kindling in the base. Fill the chimney 3/4 full with well-marinated briquets and top it off with a few untreated ones. Start the fire at the base of the chimney and, once all the briquets have been ignited, remove the chimney and build up the fire from there.

Once the fire has caught it is important to waste no time in laying on as many more coals as you need, without smothering it. At this stage flames can be allowed, but as the fire settles they will subside and the coals will be at full heat when a thin layer of grey ash covers them. You should remember that what you must aim for is a *level* spread of coals, equally hot, and covering an area preferably a little larger than the area of the food on the grill above.

When spit cooking, the fire must be stoked rather more heavily than usual and then split in two by a drip pan in a furrow down the length of the spit. Another method is to bank up the fire along one side of the fire-pan parallel to the spit but a little away from it, so that the fire-pan can be placed slightly off-centre in the direction in which the spit is revolving. In doing this, it must be remembered that the fire must be lighted about 30 to 45 minutes in advance, depending on the type of fuel used.

Remember also that, while beginners are inclined to use too many coals, it is important to lay a deeper foundation to the fire and to have more coals warming on the side ready to put on it if the cooking is going to last some time, for a grill is put completely out of action the moment the fire is covered with fresh coals. At all events, until some experience has been gained it is better to waste a little fuel than to spoil good food.

For those who like to add aromatic flavours, such as fresh herbs, a few bay leaves, sticks of fruitwood, hickory or juniper or a couple of cloves of garlic, they should be added towards the end of the cooking time.

Setting the scene

Almost any garden or patio can become a barbecue party area with a little imagination. As barbecues are 'fun' parties the setting needs to be informal and this is always easier out of doors. Decorations help, especially after dark, and though they need not be too elaborate bright colours, mystic lights, lanterns, balloons and background music help set the mood. Choose a *theme*, depending on the age of your guests – a cowboy on the range for children, a discothèque for teenagers and for adults a South Seas atmosphere with moonlight, draped netting and appropriate music. Should there be no moon on the night of your party make one with a large round of cardboard covered with crinkled foil, hang it high in a tree with perhaps a flickering light nearby. To make it all stand out against the sky, trees and houses an outdoor decoration must be conspicuous; the bigger, the bolder, the brighter, the better!

Guests often tend to cluster unless you encourage them to move around. The lure of food and drink is a good way to keep people moving, a crisp here, a crudité there, dips and dunks somewhere else. Small tables to hold these tit-bits can be made from empty orange boxes, up-ended and covered with a bright cloth. Depending on the amount of room available spread things out as much as possible – dancing, food and drink each in a different area so guests have to mingle.

On a chilly night try a fire in an old metal wheelbarrow or large bucket, or small charcoal braziers dotted around on tables. The braziers can also be used for guests to cook their own kebabs. A bright cheerful glow is very effective in livening a group of guests. Lighting is important, not too much to flood-light the place but enough for guests to see where they are going and what they are eating. Large torches and spot lights placed in trees and bushes make good party lights and fairy lights strung from tree to tree add a touch of magic to the setting. Candles are attractive and give flickering glows but they usually need some protection from the wind. In a sheltered spot candles in bottles can be used, but on tables use large dumpy candles or night lights in pottery containers. The sides of the containers will afford some protection. Empty cans, which have a pattern of holes punched all round, make good sturdy candle holders too.

The first thing to greet your guests should be the bar, located away from the entrance and the cooking area to avoid congestion. An attractive bar can be made with a trestle table, a bamboo pole placed at each corner for uprights and reed matting, canvas or crêpe paper for a canopy above, draped from pole to pole.

Music is a must at a party, it can do as much in setting the party atmosphere as the decorations you use. Try hiding a portable record-player behind shrubbery, loud enough for your guests, but not too loud for your neighbours. Why not invite them too?

Remember that guests at a barbecue usually eat and drink heartily so have plenty of food and drink. The barbecue area should be convenient-ly close to the kitchen for fetching and carrying and to run an electric extension cord from the kitchen to the spit/rotisserie motor or an electric starter (if necessary) and for an outdoor spot light, which can be fastened up high to shine on to the cooking area. In addition to the cooking area you will need a table for the raw food and the aids and accessories required for the barbecuing, these can be covered with foil to keep off the dust and flies.

Set a little aside from the cooking area, you will need two tables – a large one for the barbecued food, salads, vegetables, hot bread or rolls, and the other for the desserts. The serving tables can have large lawn or beach umbrellas placed nearby. Shine a spot-light from the ground on to the underneath of the umbrella so your guests can see what there is to eat. Tables covered with paper cloths or gaily coloured crêpe paper should be dotted about for guests to sit at. If it is a windy evening keep the cloths in place with pegs round the sides of the table.

Your precious china, crystal and cutlery would look out of place in the open, and could get broken or might even get cleared away with the rubbish. Instead use paper cloths and serviettes, paper or plastic plates (very attractive matching sets are available now) and this could help to set your party theme. Paper or plastic mugs or cups are not liked by everyone for drinking and even the cheapest 'vino' will taste better out of glasses, so why not buy some cheap glasses just for use in the garden.

Do have lots of serviettes or kitchen rolls about the place as many barbecued foods will be eaten with the fingers. A tiered trolley is useful as a 'sweet' server but also very useful for clearing away after the eating and drinking is over. Do not forget the coffee pots – these can be kept hot on the side of the barbecue or on small home-made barbecues (see p 23) or the hot coffee can be put into thermos jugs. Happy barbecuing and happy eating!

Drinks, dips and appetizers

A great way to greet your guests is to serve a 'cup' or 'punch' as soon as they arrive, this will get them in the party mood, and then during the barbecue wine or beer can be served.

Dips, dunks and appetizers are ideal for nibbles. Keep the dunks small and crisp – use carrots, celery or cucumber together with biscuits, and crisps. Nuts, olives and gherkins will all help to keep away the pangs of hunger as the delicious smells from the barbecue waft across the garden.

DRINKS

Cider Cup

Serves 8–12

285g/10oz can pineapple chunks
125ml/¼ pint dry sherry
finely pared rind and juice of 1 orange
finely pared rind and juice of 1 lemon
1½ litres/3 pints cider
½ litre/1 pint soda water
8–12 maraschino cherries
few sprigs of mint

Empty the can of pineapple into a bowl, add the sherry, rind and juice of lemon and orange and chill for 1–2 hours. Add the chilled cider and soda water. Pour into glasses and serve topped with a cherry and a sprig of mint.

Fruit Juice Cocktail

Serves 8

125ml/¼ pint cold water
125ml/¼ pint fresh or bottled lemon juice
250ml/½ pint fresh, frozen or canned orange juice
15ml/1 tablespoon lime juice
100g/4oz caster sugar
2 egg whites
crushed ice
maraschino cherries

Put all the ingredients, except cherries, into a cocktail shaker or screw top jar. Cover and shake well for a few minutes until light and frothy. Serve in a glass with a cherry on a stick.

Glühwein
Serves 8

1 litre/2 pints red wine
150g/6oz Demerara sugar
3 sticks cinnamon
2 lemons stuck with 6 cloves
125ml/¼ pint brandy
1 orange

Put the red wine, sugar, cinnamon and lemons into a saucepan, bring to the boil, then simmer with the lid on for 2–3 minutes. Strain the liquid into a jug and add the brandy. Cut the orange into thin slices and serve with the Glühwein.

Mulled Ale
Serves 6–8

2 lemons
500ml/1 pint ale
60ml/4 tablespoons brandy
30ml/2 tablespoons rum
30ml/2 tablespoons gin
25g/1oz Demerara sugar
250ml/½ pint water
2.5ml/½ teaspoon nutmeg
2.5ml/½ teaspoon cinnamon

Peel the lemons thinly and squeeze the juice from them. Put all the ingredients into a saucepan and heat; do not boil. Strain the liquid and serve at once in punch glasses.

White Wine Cup
Serves 8–12

3 oranges
50g/2oz caster sugar
1 bottle Moselle
1 bottle sparkling Moselle
250g/8oz fresh strawberries

Slice the oranges very thinly and put into a bowl. Sprinkle over the sugar and add the Moselle wine. Cover the bowl and allow the fruit to marinate for 2 hours. Add some ice cubes and the chilled sparkling Moselle. Serve the drink garnished with the orange slices and strawberries.

China Punch
Serves 8–12

250ml/½ pint China tea
100g/4oz sugar
juice of 2 lemons
½ bottle red wine
½ bottle white wine
125ml/¼ pint rum
1 bottle sparkling white wine

Make the tea and allow to infuse for 10–15 minutes. Put the sugar and lemon juice into a bowl and strain the tea in to it; stir until the sugar has dissolved. Chill for 1 hour. Have the wines and rum well chilled and pour into the bowl. Stir well and serve.

Planters Punch

1 of bitter	1 = lemon juice
2 of sweet	2 = sugar syrup
3 of hard	3 = rum
4 of weak	4 = crushed ice
Angostura bitters to taste	

Mix all the ingredients together and shake well. Pour over more crushed ice in a glass. Garnish with a piece of pineapple and a cherry on a stick.

DIPS

Cream Cheese and Olive Dip
Serves 8

200g/8oz cream cheese
250ml/½ pint double cream
2.5ml/½ teaspoon curry powder
5ml/1 teaspoon made mustard
15ml/1 tablespoon mango chutney
 juice
salt and pepper
12 Spanish stuffed olives, halved
a little milk

Stir together the cream cheese, cream, curry powder, mustard and chutney juice until well blended. Add salt and pepper to taste. Stir in the olives, reserving a few for garnish. Add a little milk if necessary to make the correct consistency. Serve with crisps, raw vegetables and biscuits.

Piquant Dip

125ml/5fl. oz soured cream
45ml/3 tablespoons mayonnaise
few drops Tabasco
5ml/1 teaspoon made mustard
10ml/1 dessertspoon Worcestershire
 sauce
15ml/1 tablespoon horseradish
 sauce
1 clove garlic, crushed
30ml/2 tablespoons sherry
salt and pepper

Mix all the ingredients well together. Pour into a small dish and chill well before serving with raw vegetables.

Parmesan Dip

25g/1oz butter
1 large onion, chopped
285g/10oz can condensed asparagus
 soup
30ml/2 tablespoons milk
50g/2oz grated Parmesan cheese

Melt the butter in a saucepan, add the finely chopped onion and cook until soft but not brown. Stir in the soup, milk and cheese. Heat thoroughly and serve with savoury biscuits.

APPETIZERS

Guacamole
Serves 8

2 ripe avocados
1 green pepper
1 tomato
25g/1oz onion, chopped
30ml/2 tablespoons lemon juice
10ml/1 dessertspoon olive oil
2.5ml/½ teaspoon ground coriander
salt and pepper

Peel the avocados, cut in half, remove the stones and put the flesh into a basin; mash well with a fork. Cut the green pepper in half, remove the seeds and chop finely; remove the skin and pips from the tomato and chop the flesh. Add all the ingredients to the avocados and beat well until smooth. Put the mixture into a serving bowl, cover and chill for 1 hour before serving.
Serve the Guacamole with blanched cauliflower, celery sticks, carrot rings, cucumber wedges, crisps or small biscuits.

Olive and Cheese Bouchées

Makes 16 bouchées

212g/7½oz packet puff pastry
little beaten egg
50g/2oz Gruyère cheese
16 Spanish stuffed olives

Roll out the pastry to 2.5mm/⅛in thick. Cut out 3.5cm/1½in circles and mark a circle in the centre with a 1.5cm/¾in cutter. Place the circles on a baking tray, brush with a little beaten egg and bake at Gas 7 or 220°C/425°F for 7 minutes. Remove from the oven and scoop out the centres of each circle. Cut the cheese into small circles, using the 1.5cm/¾in cutter and place one in the centre of each bouchée, with an olive on top. Return to the oven for a further 5 minutes until the cheese has melted and they are a golden brown. Serve warm.

Spiced Eggs

Serves 8–12

8 eggs
50g/2oz butter
2.5ml/½ teaspoon salt
2.5ml/½ teaspoon pepper
2.5ml/½ teaspoon paprika pepper
2.5ml/½ teaspoon cinnamon

Hard boil the eggs, shell while still warm and prick the whites all over. Melt the butter in a small saucepan, add the salt, peppers and cinnamon, cook for 1 minute. Add the eggs and shaking the saucepan gently, cook until the egg whites turn a light brown. Serve the eggs, cut into quarters, with raw onion rings, tomato slices and black olives.

Cheese Mousse

10ml/1 dessertspoon gelatine
30ml/2 tablespoons hot water
50g/2oz blue cheese
125ml/5fl. oz cottage cheese
10ml/1 dessertspoon Italian salad
  dressing
250ml/½ pint soured cream
salt and pepper
carrot rings
chopped parsley

Dissolve the gelatine in the hot water. Break the blue cheese into small pieces and put into a basin. Stir in the cottage cheese, Italian dressing, soured cream, salt, pepper and dissolved gelatine. Pour into a wetted ring mould and allow to set. To serve: turn the mousse out on to a serving plate and fill the centre with the raw carrot rings and sprinkle with chopped parsley.

Kipper Pâté

Serves 6–8

150g/6oz packet frozen kipper fillets
125ml/5fl. oz natural yogurt
75g/3oz gherkins, chopped
good pinch of nutmeg
juice of 1 lemon
salt and pepper

Cook the kipper fillets according to the instructions on the packet. Remove any skin and flake the fish into a basin. Add all the other ingredients and mix well. Put the mixture into a small dish and chill well before serving with small biscuits or cheese straws.

Taramasalata

450g/1lb smoked cod's roe
50g/2oz onion, finely chopped
1 cooked potato
2 cloves garlic, crushed
50g/2oz fresh white breadcrumbs
juice of 1 lemon
125ml/¼ pint oil
salt and pepper
black olives
parsley

Put the roe into a basin and beat until smooth; stir in the onion, potato, garlic and breadcrumbs. Gradually beat in the lemon juice and oil; season to taste. Put the mixture into a serving dish, decorate with sliced olives and parsley and chill before serving with crisps and small biscuits. The mixture can be piped on to biscuits and decorated with sliced olives.

Olive and Bacon Rolls

Makes 16

16 very small button mushrooms
8 rashers streaky bacon
Spanish stuffed green olives

Wash and dry the mushrooms; remove the rind from the bacon, stretch each rasher and cut in half. Wrap a piece of bacon round each mushroom, spear with a cocktail stick and grill for about 5 minutes. Place an olive on each cocktail stick and serve warm.

Party Cheese and Walnut Ball

1 green pepper
1 red pepper
50g/2oz spring onions
4 gherkins
75g/3oz sharp cheddar cheese
75g/3oz cream cheese
50g/2oz raisins
30ml/2 tablespoons sherry
10ml/2 teaspoons Worcestershire
  sauce
100g/4oz walnuts, chopped

Cut the green and red peppers in half, remove the seeds and chop the flesh finely. Chop the spring onions and gherkins. Grate the cheddar cheese. Beat the cream cheese and cheddar cheese together until smooth. Add all the other ingredients, except the walnuts, and mix well together. Shape the mixture into a round, wrap in a piece of foil and put in the refrigerator for 2 hours. Put the chopped walnuts in a plastic bag, remove the foil from the cheese ball and put the ball in the bag. Shake well to coat the ball with the nuts. Put the ball in the centre of a plate and surround with biscuits, crisps, carrot or cucumber sticks.

Marinades, bastes and sauces

A marinade (from the French to pickle, especially in brine) is a highly seasoned mixture in which meat and fish can be soaked to give them a certain flavour, or to tenderize them, before they are cooked. Enough should be prepared in which to lay the food so that it can be turned in it from time to time, and basted with it. If the meat or fish is of a size that makes it difficult to impregnate them with the marinade by turning and basting, then place them in a plastic bag and seal it tightly. It is easier then to turn the bag over from time to time to achieve the same effect.

In barbecuing, some marinades can also be used to baste with while cooking and, even after that, as a sauce. Most marinades contain acid (from vinegar, wine or citrus juice) which acts as a tenderizer, fat (from oil or butter) to add moisture to very lean meats, and seasonings to add flavour.

A baste is brushed on as the food is cooking and so does not penetrate as a marinade does. The main role of basting is to preserve surface moisture, and in certain cases to produce a glazing effect. It is absolutely essential when spit cooking to baste constantly.

Sauces may be related to marinades and bastes and, indeed, may be left-overs of these but, if prepared separately, care should be taken to make sure they blend, and so do not detract from or conflict with the marinades or bastes used on the food before and during cooking. A good stand-by is seasoned butter which can be spread over the food as it melts.

MARINADES

Sweet and Sour Marinade *for*
chicken, pork or ham

125ml/¼ pint orange juice
125ml/¼ pint dry white wine
65ml/2½fl. oz white wine vinegar
30ml/2 tablespoons oil
25g/1oz onion, chopped
15ml/1 tablespoon soy sauce
25g/1oz Demerara sugar
juice of ½ lemon
2.5ml/½ teaspoon celery salt
ground black pepper

Mix all the ingredients together in a screw top jar, cover and shake well. Leave for 1 hour for the flavours to blend and then pour over the prepared meat and leave to marinate for several hours, or overnight in the refrigerator.

White Wine Marinade *for fish or chicken*

125ml/¼ pint oil
250ml/½ pint white wine
salt and ground black pepper
50g/2oz onion, chopped
1 clove garlic, crushed
1 bay leaf
25g/1oz chives, chopped
25g/1oz parsley, chopped

Mix all the ingredients together in a screw top jar, cover and shake well to blend. Pour over the fish or chicken and leave to marinate for 2–3 hours.

Lamb Marinade

250ml/½ pint dry red wine
125ml/¼ pint oil
1 clove garlic, crushed
10ml/1 dessertspoon dried rosemary
6 cloves
salt and ground black pepper
15ml/1 tablespoon chopped parsley

Mix all the ingredients well together, pour over the prepared lamb, cover and leave to marinate for 1–2 hours. 10ml/1 dessertspoon of chopped mint can be used in place of the rosemary.

Red Wine Marinade *for beef or game*

250ml/½ pint oil
250ml/½ pint red wine
2 cloves garlic, crushed
25g/1oz onion, finely chopped
salt and ground black pepper
1 bay leaf
5ml/1 teaspoon basil
2.5ml/½ teaspoon oregano

Mix all the ingredients together in a screw top jar, cover and shake well. Pour over the prepared meat and leave to marinate.

BASTES

Californian Barbecue Baste

125ml/¼ pint oil
125ml/¼ pint red wine
125ml/¼ pint pineapple juice
5ml/1 teaspoon chopped parsley
salt and ground black pepper
2 cloves garlic, crushed

Mix all the ingredients together and use to baste the food during cooking.

Orange and Garlic Baste

(3 kilos/6lbs ribs)
Serves 8

This mixture can be poured over the ribs to marinate and then brushed on the ribs during the cooking on the grill.

250ml/$\frac{1}{2}$ pint orange juice
250ml/$\frac{1}{2}$ pint oil
60ml/4 tablespoons marmalade
4 cloves garlic, crushed
60ml/4 tablespoons vinegar
20ml/2 dessertspoons Worcestershire sauce
salt and pepper

Mix together all the ingredients, pour over the ribs, leave to marinate for up to 24 hours, then drain and grill.

Lemon Barbecue Baste

Delicious as a marinade and a baste for chicken pieces and as a baste for a whole chicken on the spit.

125ml/$\frac{1}{4}$ pint oil
125ml/$\frac{1}{4}$ pint lemon juice
1 clove garlic, crushed
2.5ml/$\frac{1}{2}$ teaspoon salt
ground black pepper
25g/1oz onion, finely chopped
2.5ml/$\frac{1}{2}$ teaspoon tarragon

Put all the ingredients together in a screw top jar, cover and shake well. Leave overnight to blend the flavours.

Mustard and Honey Baste

Use to brush on ham or burgers while cooking

100g/4oz Demerara sugar
15ml/1 tablespoon dry mustard
30ml/2 tablespoons vinegar
30ml/2 tablespoons clear honey
250ml/$\frac{1}{2}$ pint pineapple juice

Mix all the ingredients together in a small saucepan, heat to dissolve the sugar, then simmer for 5 minutes.

SAUCES

Barbecue Tomato Sauce

60ml/4 tablespoons wine vinegar
60ml/4 tablespoons water
75ml/5 tablespoons tomato ketchup
25g/1oz Demerara sugar
15ml/1 tablespoon Worcestershire sauce
salt and pepper

Mix all the ingredients together in a small saucepan, bring to the boil and simmer for 10 minutes.

Tipsy Cheese Sauce

Good to serve with grilled sausages and steaks

100g/4oz strong cheddar cheese
125ml/$\frac{1}{4}$ pint sherry
5ml/1 teaspoon dry mustard
1 clove garlic, crushed
salt and ground black pepper

Melt the cheese slowly in a saucepan. Gradually stir in the sherry then add the other ingredients and heat a further 2–3 minutes.

Hawaiian Sauce

(3 kilos/6lbs ribs)
Serves 8

This sauce can be used to brush over the ribs during cooking and then separately as a sauce or dip with the cooked ribs.

50g/2oz Demerara sugar
30ml/2 tablespoons tomato purée
2 cloves garlic, crushed
30ml/2 tablespoons soy sauce
125ml/¼ pint sherry
125ml/¼ pint oil
45ml/3 tablespoons lemon juice
20ml/2 dessertspoons Worcestershire
  sauce
60ml/4 tablespoons wine vinegar
2 × 285g/10oz cans crushed pineapple

Mix all the ingredients well together and use as a baste on the ribs after they have cooked for about 10 minutes on the grill.

Honey and Sherry Sauce

(3 kilos/6lbs ribs)
Serves 8

This mixture can be used as a marinade over the ribs, and as a baste during cooking.

125ml/¼ pint oil
125ml/¼ pint wine vinegar
125ml/¼ pint sherry
60ml/4 tablespoons clear honey
salt and pepper

Mix all the ingredients well together and pour over the ribs. Leave to marinate for up to 24 hours. The mixture can also be brushed on the ribs during cooking.

Mustard Sauce

This sauce is good to serve with hot dogs, sausages or frankfurters

10ml/1 dessertspoon dry mustard
30ml/2 tablespoons cold water
50g/2oz butter
50g/2oz onion, finely chopped
125ml/¼ pint dry white wine
30ml/2 tablespoons brown sauce
15ml/1 tablespoon clear honey
juice of 1 lemon
salt and ground black pepper

Blend the mustard and water together. Melt the butter in a small saucepan, add the chopped onion and fry 2–3 minutes. Add the wine and simmer for 4–5 minutes. Stir in the brown sauce, honey, lemon juice and season to taste. Remove the saucepan from the heat and stir in the blended mustard.

Raisin Sauce

Delicious to serve with barbecued ham

50g/2oz butter
25g/1oz flour
250ml/½ pint stock
50g/2oz seedless raisins
25g/1oz flaked almonds
1.25ml/¼ teaspoon ground cloves
1.25ml/¼ teaspoon ground cinnamon
65ml/2½fl. oz sherry
finely grated rind and juice of 1
  lemon

Melt the butter, add the flour and cook the roux for a few minutes until a golden brown. Gradually stir in the stock, bring to the boil and simmer for 2–3 minutes. Add all the other ingredients and simmer a further 3 minutes.

Zesty Horseradish Sauce

Delicious served with steaks or hamburgers and as a topping for jacket potatoes

125ml/¼ pint double cream
juice of 1 lemon
5ml/1 teaspoon horseradish sauce
10ml/2 teaspoons Worcestershire
  sauce
2 spring onions, finely chopped

Mix together all the ingredients and leave to stand for 4 hours before using.

Bitter Orange Sauce

Use as a baste for ham during cooking or as a sauce for serving with ham

100g/4oz bitter marmalade
juice of 2 lemons
15ml/1 tablespoon brown sugar
50g/2oz raisins

Put all the ingredients into a small saucepan and simmer for 5 minutes.

Sweet and Sour Sauce

Use as a marinade and for basting pork, ham or chicken

250ml/½ pint light beer
75g/3oz orange marmalade
45ml/3 tablespoons soy sauce
25g/1oz Demerara sugar
10ml/1 dessertspoon dry mustard
5ml/1 teaspoon ground ginger
2.5ml/½ teaspoon salt
few drops Tabasco

Mix all the ingredients together in a screw top jar, cover and shake well until blended.

Hot Barbecue Sauce

Use as a baste and a sauce

30ml/2 tablespoons oil
50g/2oz onion, chopped
50g/2oz celery, chopped
1 clove garlic, crushed
210g/7½oz can tomatoes
30ml/2 tablespoons tomato purée
45ml/3 tablespoons vinegar
15ml/1 tablespoon Worcestershire
  sauce
few drops Tabasco
10ml/1 dessertspoon chilli powder
125ml/¼ pint stock
salt and ground black pepper
2.5ml/½ teaspoon paprika pepper

Heat the oil in a saucepan, add the onion and celery and fry for 4–5 minutes. Stir in all the other ingredients and simmer for 20–25 minutes.

Piquant Dressing

45ml/3 tablespoons wine vinegar
finely grated rind and juice of 1
  lemon
5ml/1 teaspoon dry mustard
1 clove garlic, crushed
125ml/¼ pint oil
salt and pepper
5ml/1 teaspoon dried basil

Mix all the ingredients together in a screw top jar and shake well.

Sour Cream Apple Sauce

250ml/½ pint soured cream
2 hard green eating apples, grated
30ml/2 tablespoons horseradish
  sauce
salt and ground black pepper

Mix all the ingredients well together about ½ hour before serving.

Fish

Most fish can be cooked on a barbecue and especially good, because of their high fat content, are trout, mackerel and herring. All fish need to be handled carefully as they can break up so easily; it needs to be fully but not overcooked as this will cause the fish to be dry. The fish can be wrapped in foil with butter or put into a greased grill basket so that it can be turned over easily. If the fish is cooked without foil do baste it frequently to keep the fish moist during cooking, either with the baste given in the recipe or just melted butter to which you have added a little lemon juice.

Sole Turnovers
Serves 8

8 fillets of sole
salt and pepper
2.5ml/½ teaspoon basil
8 slices processed cheese
100g/4oz butter, melted
65ml/2½fl. oz white wine
lemon wedges
watercress

Wash and dry the fish, sprinkle with salt, pepper and basil. Place a slice of cheese on each fillet and fold in half. Mix together the butter and wine and brush over the fish. Put the fish in a well greased wire grill basket and cook on the grill over hot coals for 6–8 minutes, turning once and basting frequently with the butter. Serve garnished with the lemon and watercress.

Fish Parcels
Serves 8

8 fillets of white fish
salt and pepper
100g/4oz mushrooms
100g/4oz onions, chopped
25g/1oz capers
50g/2oz butter
250ml/½ pint single cream

Wash and dry the fish. Put each fillet on a double thickness of buttered foil and sprinkle with salt and pepper. Wash and slice the mushrooms. Arrange the mushrooms, onions and capers on the fish and dot with butter. Pour over the cream. Wrap the foil loosely over the fish to make a neat parcel. Cook on the grill over hot coals for 25–30 minutes. Serve the fish on a dish with the juices and sprinkle with chopped parsley.

50

Peppy Cod Steaks

Serves 8

8 cod steaks
125ml/¼ pint oil
65ml/2½fl. oz lemon juice
salt and pepper
125ml/¼ pint tomato ketchup
15ml/1 tablespoon chilli sauce
45ml/3 tablespoons lemon juice
15ml/1 tablespoon horseradish sauce
30ml/2 tablespoons mayonnaise
10ml/1 dessertspoon Worcestershire
  sauce
salt and pepper
few drops Tabasco sauce

Wash and dry the fish. Mix together the oil, 65ml/2½fl. oz lemon juice and seasoning. Put the fish on to a well greased barbecue grill or in greased fish grills (see page 31), baste with the mixture and cook the fish over medium coals for 8 minutes, brush again with the baste, turn the fish, baste again and cook a further 8–10 minutes. Mix together the tomato ketchup, chilli sauce, 45ml/3 tablespoons lemon juice, horseradish sauce, mayonnaise, Worcestershire sauce and salt and pepper. Place the fish on a serving dish and pour over the sauce.

Special Barbecued Lobsters

Serves 8

4 lobsters
100g/4oz butter
2 cloves garlic, crushed
juice of 1 lemon
salt and pepper
watercress
lemon wedges

Split the lobsters in half lengthwise and remove the intestine, stomach and gills. Remove the flesh from the claws and add to the flesh in the shells. Melt the butter, add the garlic, lemon juice, salt and pepper and brush the lobsters with this sauce. Cook the lobsters on the grill over medium coals for 12–15 minutes, basting several times with the sauce. Place them on a serving dish and garnish with watercress and lemon.

Smoky Mackerel

Serves 8

8 mackerel
125ml/¼ pint wine vinegar
65ml/2½fl. oz oil
65ml/2½fl. oz lemon juice
25g/1oz brown sugar
salt and pepper
15ml/1 tablespoon Worcestershire
  sauce
2 bay leaves
2.5ml/½ teaspoon paprika pepper
8 sprigs of rosemary

Remove the heads from the fish, gut, wash well and put into a shallow dish. In a small saucepan mix together all the other ingredients, except the rosemary, and bring to the boil; allow to cool then pour over the fish, leave to marinate for 30 minutes. Place the fish in a well-greased, hinged wire grill, each with a piece of rosemary on top and cook on the grill over medium coals for 8 minutes, baste with the remaining sauce, turn and cook a further 8–12 minutes. Serve the fish garnished with lemon and parsley.

Red mullet and trout can be cooked in the same way.

Simple Salmon Cutlets
Serves 8

8 salmon steaks
100g/4oz butter, melted
juice of 2 lemons
salt and pepper
savoury butter, see page 102
lemon wedges

Put the salmon on a well greased hinged wire grill. Mix together the butter, lemon juice, salt and pepper. Brush the salmon with this baste and cook over hot coals for 10–12 minutes, turning once but basting frequently during cooking with the butter mixture. Top each cutlet with savoury butter and garnish with lemon wedges. If a wire grill is not available wrap each cutlet in greased foil with some of the baste and cook on the barbecue grill for 15–20 minutes, turning once during cooking.

Herbed Herrings
Serves 8

8 herrings
100g/4oz butter
salt and pepper
5ml/1 teaspoon coriander seeds
2.5ml/½ teaspoon cardamon
finely grated rind and juice of 2
  lemons
250ml/10fl. oz natural yogurt

Remove the heads, gut and wash the fish well. Melt the butter in a small saucepan, add all the other ingredients and brush the fish well with this mixture. Place the fish in a flat wire basket and cook on the grill over hot coals, turning and basting frequently, for 25–30 minutes. Serve on a bed of chopped lettuce with lemon wedges.

Stuffed Trout
Serves 8

8 trout
salt and pepper
150g/6oz crab meat
50g/2oz fresh white breadcrumbs
5ml/1 teaspoon fish seasoning
50g/2oz butter, melted

Gut and wash the trout and sprinkle the inside with salt and pepper. Mix together the crab, breadcrumbs and seasoning and use to fill the cavity. Place each trout on a piece of buttered foil, brush with melted butter and bring the edges of the foil together to make a loose parcel. Place the parcels on the grill over medium coals and cook for 25–30 minutes. Open the parcels carefully, serve the trout on a dish with the buttery juices and lemon wedges.

Trout with Almonds
Serves 8

8 trout
100g/4oz butter
salt and pepper
grated rind and juice of 2 lemons
100g/4oz toasted flaked almonds
chopped parsley

Gut the trout and wash well. Put each trout on to a square of buttered foil. Dot with butter and sprinkle with salt, pepper, lemon rind and juice. Bring the ends of the foil together and seal loosely. Place the foil parcels on the grill and cook over hot coals for 25–30 minutes, turning once during cooking. Open the parcels carefully, place the trout on a serving dish, pour over the buttery juices and sprinkle with almonds and parsley.

Barbecued Sprats

Serves 8

1 kilo/2lbs sprats
75g/3oz flour
oil
lemon wedges
fried parsley

Wash and dry the sprats, toss in flour and brush with oil. Put them on the well-greased grill of the barbecue or in a greased, hinged, grill basket and cook over hot coals for 4–6 minutes, turning once and brushing again with oil. Serve garnished with lemon and fried parsley.

Fried Parsley

You will need a lot of parsley as it shrivels up in frying. Remove the stalks and wash the parsley. Dry it very thoroughly on kitchen paper and put it in a small mesh wire basket; plunge into a deep pan of hot oil for a few seconds. Turn on to clean kitchen paper to drain.

Corn-Husk Cooked Trout

If corn husks are available these can be used in place of the foil. After washing and gutting the trout place them in the corn husk (this is the outside part of the corn on the cob after the corn has been removed), brush the trout with melted butter and bring the husk round the fish; tie at the silk end. Put the husks in hot coals and cook for 12–15 minutes, turning once during cooking. Remove the husks and serve the trout with lemon wedges.

Sausages and burgers

The great British 'banger' must be included in any barbecue especially where guests cook their own food. Great fun can be had cooking sausages on wetted sticks over the coals but they can also be cooked on the grill or wrapped in foil and cooked directly in the coals.

Do not prick sausages before cooking and they should never be prodded during cooking. Blanching sausages first is an ideal way to seal in the flavour and goodness. Just put them in boiling water and simmer gently for 4 minutes; take out, drain on kitchen paper and use in your favourite barbecue recipe.

Sausages can be threaded lengthways on to skewers for easy handling and to prevent chipolata sausages from slipping through the grill. Diagonal cuts can be made in the sausages to prevent them curling up during cooking. They should be brushed with oil and turned frequently during cooking; basting with a sauce can be done at the 'turning stage' and not at the initial cooking stage, otherwise they can easily burn.

Hot dogs and frankfurters are already cooked so only need a short time to heat through and get the barbecue flavour.

Burgers – so popular with children – can be 'dressed up' to become appetizing and filling for adults when served in warm buns with fried onions, tomatoes and pickles.

Burgers – popularly called Hamburgers in America – were called Viennese steaks in Victorian times in this country; whatever the name, burgers can be made with all types of minced meat.

54

SAUSAGES

Barbecued Sausages with Sweet and Sour Sauce
Serves 8

1 kilo/2lbs large sausages
16 small onions, peeled

Thread the sausages on long skewers with the onions in between. Cook on the grill over hot coals, turning frequently, for 12–15 minutes. Serve with corn-on-the-cob, crusty bread and sweet and sour sauce.

Beans and Frankfurters
Serves 8

30ml/2 tablespoons oil
50g/2oz onion, chopped
820g/29oz can baked beans
425g/15oz can pineapple chunks
16 frankfurters

Heat the oil in a frying pan, add the onion and fry for 3–4 minutes. Stir in the baked beans and cook a further 2–3 minutes. Drain the pineapple and cut each frankfurter into 4 pieces. Thread pineapple and frankfurters alternately on 8 skewers. Divide the bean mixture between 8 squares of double thickness foil, place a skewer on top and twist the foil together to make a loose parcel. Put the parcels on the grill and cook over hot coals for 10–15 minutes. To serve: put a parcel on a plate, open the foil and tuck it underneath the plate.

Turkish Sausages
Serves 8

1 kilo/2lbs chipolata sausages
½ litre/1 pint natural yogurt
grated rind and juice of 1 lemon
salt and pepper
50g/2oz onion, chopped
5ml/1 teaspoon ground ginger
10ml/2 teaspoons curry powder
30ml/2 tablespoons chopped mint

Put the sausages into a shallow dish. Mix together all the other ingredients and pour over the sausages. Cover and leave to marinate in the refrigerator for 12 hours. Remove the sausages from the marinade and cook on the grill over hot coals for 10–12 minutes, turning frequently. Heat the marinade to serve as a sauce with the sausages and cucumber salad, mango chutney, toasted nuts and desiccated coconut.

Sausage in a Blanket
Serves 8

8 large sausages
little chutney
8 rashers streaky bacon

Cook the sausages on the grill over hot coals for 7–8 minutes, turning frequently. Make a cut the length of the sausage, open out and fill with chutney. Remove the rind from the bacon and wrap a rasher round each sausage; return to the grill and cook for a further 7–8 minutes, turning frequently during cooking. In place of the chutney put a wedge of cheese.

Piquant Sausages
Serves 8

450g/1lb chipolata sausages
French mustard
16 long soft rolls
lettuce

Make 3 diagonal slits in each sausage and spread the mustard over the sausages; cook on the grill over hot coals for 8–12 minutes, turning frequently during cooking. Meanwhile wrap the rolls in foil and heat in the coals; split them and arrange lettuce and sausages in each one.

Barbecued Sausages
Serves 8

50g/2oz butter
100g/4oz onion, chopped
226g/8oz can tomatoes
30ml/2 tablespoons tomato ketchup
30ml/2 tablespoons vinegar
30ml/2 tablespoons Demerara sugar
10ml/2 teaspoons dry mustard
30ml/2 tablespoons Worcestershire
  sauce
450g/1lb sausages
200g/8oz cooked rice

Melt the butter in a frying pan, add the onions and fry 3–4 minutes. Add all the other ingredients, except sausages and rice, and simmer on the grill over medium coals for 15–20 minutes. Meanwhile cook the sausages on the grill over medium coals for 12–16 minutes, turning frequently during cooking. Serve the sausages on the rice with the sauce poured over and sprinkle with chopped parsley.

Frankly Quick Crisp
Serves 8

16 frankfurters
50g/2oz cornflakes
2.5ml/$\frac{1}{2}$ teaspoon salt
25g/1oz flour
2.5ml/$\frac{1}{2}$ teaspoon curry powder
1 egg
Sour Cream Apple sauce, see page 49

Cut each frankfurter in half. Crush the cornflakes and put in a plastic bag. Add the salt, flour and curry powder, shake well to mix together. Beat the egg in a dish, add the frankfurter pieces and then drop the pieces into the plastic bag and coat with the cornflake mixture; shake surplus mixture off then put the frankfurters on the grill and cook over hot coals for 6–8 minutes, turning frequently during cooking.

Savoury Herb Patties
Serves 8

400g/1lb sausage meat
10ml/2 teaspoons basil
100g/4oz bacon, chopped
1 onion, grated
salt and pepper
pinch dry mustard
2 egg yolks
25g/1oz butter, melted

Mix all the ingredients together, except butter, and shape into 8 small patties. Brush with melted butter and cook on the grill over medium coals for 10–12 minutes, turning and basting with butter several times during cooking. Serve in a toasted bun topped with raw onion and tomato slices.

Hot Dogs Hawaiian

Serves 8

45ml/3 tablespoons oil
100g/4oz onion, chopped
30ml/2 tablespoons cornflour
10ml/1 dessertspoon curry powder
5ml/1 teaspoon salt
285g/10oz can crushed pineapple
30ml/2 tablespoons vinegar
16 hot dogs

Heat the oil in a frying pan, add the onion and fry for 4–5 minutes. Mix together the cornflour, curry powder and salt and stir into the onion. Add the pineapple and vinegar and cook over low coals, stirring all the time, until the mixture thickens, simmer 2–3 minutes. Put the hot dogs on the grill of the barbecue and heat over hot coals for 5 minutes, then arrange them on a serving dish and pour the sauce over.

BURGERS

Mushroom and Bacon Burgers

Serves 8

200g/8oz mushrooms
50g/2oz butter
1 kilo/2lbs minced beef
2 eggs
50g/2oz plain flour
50g/2oz onion, chopped
1 clove garlic, crushed
2.5ml/½ teaspoon barbecue seasoning
salt and pepper
8 rashers streaky bacon

Wash and slice the mushrooms. Melt the butter in a frying pan, add the mushrooms and fry 4–5 minutes. Mix together all the other ingredients, except the bacon, and divide into 16 portions. Shape each portion into a thin burger and cover 8 burgers with the mushrooms. Cover with another burger and press the edges well together to seal. Remove the rinds from the bacon and wrap a slice round the edges of each burger. Secure with a wooden tooth pick. Cook the burgers on the grill over hot coals for 10–12 minutes, turning once during cooking. If liked, they can be brushed with a barbecue sauce during cooking. Serve in a bap.

Tuna Burgers

Serves 8

2 198g/7oz cans tuna fish
2 onions, finely chopped
100g/4oz celery, chopped
15ml/1 tablespoon capers, chopped
15ml/1 tablespoon chopped parsley
10ml/1 dessertspoon Worcestershire
   sauce
50g/2oz fresh white breadcrumbs
salt and pepper
finely grated rind and juice of 1
   lemon
oil for brushing
8 buns

Empty the tuna and oil into a basin and mash well. Add all the other ingredients, except oil and buns, and mix well together. Shape into 8 burgers and cook on the greased grill over medium coals for 12–15 minutes, brushing with oil and turning several times during cooking. Split the buns in half and toast them. Serve a burger in each bun with lettuce and sliced tomato.

Matadors' Beefburgers

Serves 8

2 large onions
30ml/2 tablespoons oil
8 beefburgers
40 Spanish stuffed green olives
30ml/2 tablespoons tomato chutney
8 soft baps
8 cocktail sticks

Peel and slice the onion in rings. Heat the oil in a frying pan add the onion and fry until soft and a golden brown. Drain and keep hot. Brush the beef-burgers with a little oil and cook on the grill over hot coals for 12–15 minutes, turning and brushing with more oil during cooking. Chop 16 olives, keep the remainder for decoration. Mix together the chopped olives and chutney. Cut the baps in half, spread with the chutney, put one beefburger on each, cover with onion rings, and replace top of bap. Thread the remaining olives on the cocktail sticks, 3 on each, pimento stuffing showing sideways, and spear into the top of the bap.

Mr Perrins' Sausage Burgers

Serves 8

1 kilo/2lbs sausagemeat
30ml/2 tablespoons Worcestershire sauce
1 onion, chopped
50g/2oz fresh white breadcrumbs
1 egg
salt and pepper
8 soft baps
sliced onion rings
sliced tomatoes

Mix together the sausagemeat, Worcestershire sauce, chopped onion, breadcrumbs, egg and seasoning. Shape into 8 flat cakes about 7.5cm/3in in diameter. Cook on the grill over medium coals for 12–15 minutes turning once. Split the baps and toast the cut side. Put a burger on a bap and top with the onion and tomato slices.

Cheesy Topped Burgers

Serves 8

100g/4oz butter
100g/4oz blue cheese
1 kilo/2lbs lamb, cut from the shoulder
50g/2oz onion, chopped
30ml/2 tablespoons tomato ketchup
30ml/2 tablespoons Worcestershire sauce
50g/2oz fresh white breadcrumbs
5ml/1 teaspoon dried mint
salt and pepper
25g/1oz flour

Cream the butter, crumble the cheese and beat into the butter, form into a roll, wrap in foil and put in the refrigerator until required. Mince the lamb and add the onion, tomato ketchup, Worcestershire sauce, breadcrumbs, mint and salt and pepper to taste. Shape the mixture into 8 burgers and coat with a little flour. Cook the burgers on the grill over hot coals for 12–18 minutes, turning once during cooking. Just before serving put a 'round' of the butter roll on to each burger.

Quick Barbecue Beefburgers

Serves 8

8 frozen beefburgers
Barbecue Tomato sauce, see page 47
8 baps

Cook the burgers on the grill over hot coals for 12–18 minutes, turning several times, and basting with the sauce frequently. Wrap the baps in foil and heat in the coals; split the baps and put a burger in each. Serve the remainder of the sauce separately. The burgers can be topped with a slice of processed cheese a few minutes before they are ready to serve.

Surprise Hamburgers

Serves 8

1 kilo/2lbs minced beef
salt and pepper
French mustard
1 large onion
8 soft baps
tomato ketchup

Mix together the meat, salt and pepper. Shape into 16 thin burgers about 7.5cm/3in in diameter and spread half with mustard. Peel and slice the onion into rings and arrange them on the mustard. Place a second burger on top and press the edges very well together. Cook on the grill over hot coals for 12–15 minutes, turning once during cooking. Split and toast the baps and spread one half with ketchup; put a burger inside and serve.
Cheese or ham slices can be used in place of the onion rings.

Lamburgers with Pineapple

Serves 8

$\frac{3}{4}$ kilo/1$\frac{1}{2}$lbs minced lamb
2 carrots, grated
2 onions, finely chopped
1 clove garlic, crushed
1 green pepper, finely chopped
1 egg
15ml/1 tablespoon chopped parsley
15ml/1 tablespoon brown sauce
salt and pepper
8 pineapple slices

Mix all the ingredients, except the pineapple, together and shape into 8 flat rounds. Cook the burgers over hot coals for 15–18 minutes, turning and brushing with oil during cooking. Just before serving top each burger with a pineapple slice and cook a further 2 minutes. Serve in toasted hamburger buns.

Kebabs, satés, brochettes, kabobs, shish kebab and anticuchos

What fun a name can be! But they all add up to the same thing – food cooked on skewers. It really is the most versatile and inexpensive method of barbecuing – a little of a lot of foods goes a long way.

Skewer cooking is ideal for do-it-yourself parties. Your guests can help themselves to the combination of foods that they enjoy most. Skewers should have wooden handles, be as long as possible and flat not round, so that the food does not slip when turned. If preparing the skewers in advance try to assemble them with foods that take about the same length of time to cook. Skewers can be cooked over the simplest form of home-made barbecue in the garden, on the beach or at a picnic. Remember, tightly packed skewers cook more slowly, and always baste the food well and turn frequently during cooking.

Spicy New Zealand Kebabs
Serves 8

1 kilo/2lbs lamb, cut from the leg or shoulder
125ml/¼ pint red wine
15ml/1 tablespoon tomato ketchup
15ml/1 tablespoon wine vinegar
10ml/1 dessertspoon Worcestershire sauce
25g/1oz finely chopped onion
salt and black pepper
pinch of cayenne pepper
16 button mushrooms
1 green pepper
1 red pepper
50g/2oz butter, melted

Cut the lamb into 2.5cm/1in cubes and put into a dish. Mix together the wine, ketchup, vinegar, Worcestershire sauce, onion, salt and pepper. Pour over the lamb, cover and allow to marinate for 12 hours, turning occasionally so that all the meat is covered with the marinade. Wash the mushrooms. Cut the peppers in half, remove the seeds and cut each pepper into 8 pieces. Thread the lamb, mushrooms, red and green pepper on to skewers and brush with the melted butter. Cook on the grill over hot coals for 10–12 minutes, turning frequently and basting with the marinade.

Maryland Kebabs
Serves 8

50g/2oz soft brown sugar
30ml/2 tablespoons Worcestershire
 sauce
juice of 2 lemons
salt and pepper
6 chicken breasts
16 small onions
8 rashers streaky bacon
4 bananas
2 red peppers

Mix together the sugar, Worcestershire sauce, lemon juice and salt and pepper. Cut the chicken into 2.5cm/1in pieces, put into a dish and pour the marinade over. Cover and leave to marinate for 6–8 hours. At cooking time peel the onions. Remove the rinds and cut the bacon rashers in half. Peel the bananas and cut each into 4 pieces, wrap a piece of bacon round a piece of banana. Cut the peppers in half, remove the seeds and cut the flesh into 2.5cm/1in pieces. Assemble the skewers with chicken, onions, wrapped bananas and peppers. Brush with the marinade and cook on the grill over hot coals for 10–12 minutes, turning frequently and basting with the marinade. Serve on a bed of cooked rice.

Souvlakia – Kebabs from Greece
Serves 8

1 kilo/2lbs lamb, cut from the leg
16 large bay leaves
30ml/2 tablespoons oil
juice of 1 lemon
5ml/1 teaspoon oregano
salt and pepper

Cut the lamb into pieces the size of a walnut. Break each bay leaf into 4 pieces. Mix together the oil, lemon juice, oregano, salt and pepper. Thread the lamb on to skewers with pieces of bay leaf in between, allow one skewer per person. Put the skewers into a shallow dish and pour the marinade over. Leave for 1 hour. Cook the skewers on the grill over hot coals, turning frequently, for 7–10 minutes. Serve with lemon wedges and a salad.

Kebabs with Olives
Serves 8

8 rashers streaky bacon
1 kilo/2lbs rump steak
16 small tomatoes
16 button mushrooms
16 Spanish olives
little oil
300g/12oz long grain rice, cooked
 and drained
Barbecue Tomato Sauce, see page 47

Cut the rind off the bacon and stretch the rashers with the back of a knife. Cut each in half and roll up. Trim the steak and cut into 2.5cm/1in cubes. Thread the bacon rolls and steak on to 8 small skewers. Wash the tomatoes and mushrooms and thread with the olives on to another 8 small skewers. Brush the kebabs with oil and cook on the grill for 12–15 minutes adding the skewers with the vegetables for the last 8 minutes of the cooking time. The kebabs should be brushed with oil and turned several times during cooking. Serve the kebabs on a bed of cooked rice accompanied by the sauce.

Veal and Cheese Kebabs

Serves 8

450g/1lb escalope of veal
8 rashers streaky bacon
200g/8oz cheddar cheese
16 button mushrooms
8 tomatoes
oil

Cut the veal into 2.5cm/1in squares. Remove the rind from the bacon, stretch each rasher with a knife and cut into 3 pieces. Cut the cheese into 24 cubes and wrap each in a piece of bacon. Wash the mushrooms and cut the tomatoes in half. Arrange the food on skewers, brush with a little oil and cook on the grill over hot coals for 12–15 minutes, turning frequently and basting with more oil during cooking. Serve with sour rice salad, see page 91.

Hawaiian Kebabs

Serves 8

450g/1lb gammon
450g/1lb veal
8 tomatoes
425g/15oz can pineapple chunks
25g/1oz soft brown sugar
25g/1oz butter

Cut the gammon and veal into 2.5cm/1in pieces. Cut the tomatoes in half. Drain the juice from the can of pineapple. Assemble the skewers with the gammon, veal, tomatoes and pineapple chunks. Put the skewers in a shallow dish. In a small saucepan mix together the sugar, butter and pineapple juice, heat until the sugar has melted, then pour over the skewers and allow to marinate for 30 minutes.

Cook the kebabs over hot coals for 15 minutes, turning and basting frequently.

Spiced Chicken Kebabs

Serves 8

4 chicken breasts
425g/15oz can peach slices
125ml/5fl. oz natural yogurt
2 cloves garlic, crushed
50g/2oz chopped onion
5ml/1 teaspoon ground ginger
5ml/1 teaspoon chilli powder
15ml/1 tablespoon cumin seeds
5ml/1 teaspoon salt

Remove the skin and bone from the chicken and cut the flesh into 2.5cm/1in cubes, put them in a shallow dish. Drain the juice from the can of peaches, cut each slice in half. Mix together the peach juice, yogurt, garlic, onion, ground ginger, chilli, cumin and salt, pour over the chicken, cover and leave to marinate overnight. Thread the chicken and peaches on to skewers and cook on the grill over hot coals for 8–10 minutes, turning frequently during cooking. Serve the skewers on cooked rice with a salad.

Bacon and Sausage Kebabs
Serves 8

16 large sausages
16 rashers streaky bacon
8 rings pineapple
16 small mushrooms
50g/2oz butter, melted

Twist the sausages and cut each in half. Remove the rind from the bacon, cut each rasher in half and wrap round the sausage. Cut the pineapple rings into quarters. Arrange the sausage, pineapple and mushrooms alternately on the skewers, brush with the melted butter and grill over hot coals for 8–10 minutes, turning frequently and basting with the butter.
If liked the kebabs can be brushed with mustard and honey baste, see page 47.

Indonesian Saté
Serves 8

1 kilo/2lbs boneless veal, cut from the leg or shoulder
15ml/1 tablespoon ground coriander
15ml/1 tablespoon salt
2.5ml/½ teaspoon chilli pepper
5ml/1 teaspoon ground ginger
2.5ml/½ teaspoon ground black pepper
5ml/1 teaspoon cumin seeds.
125ml/¼ pint oil
125ml/¼ pint wine vinegar
juice of 2 lemons
50g/2oz brown sugar
2 cloves garlic, crushed
2 onions, peeled and chopped

Cut the meat into 2.5cm/1in cubes. Mix together the coriander, salt, chilli pepper, ginger, black pepper and cumin seeds. Toss the meat in the seasoning mixture and put into a shallow dish. Mix together the oil, vinegar, lemon juice, sugar, garlic and onions; pour over the meat and leave to marinate for 1–2 hours. Divide the meat between 8 skewers, brush with melted butter and cook on the grill over hot coals for 10–12 minutes, turning and basting frequently. Serve with salad in Pitta Bread, see page 101.

Brochette of Pork
Serves 8

1 kilo/2lbs pork tenderloin
8 rashers streaky bacon
16 button mushrooms
50g/2oz butter, melted
fine browned breadcrumbs
chopped parsley
lemon wedges

Cut the pork into 2.5cm/1in cubes. Remove the rind from the bacon, stretch the rashers and cut each into 3 pieces. Make bacon rolls. Arrange the meat, bacon rolls and mushrooms on 8 skewers, starting and ending each with a mushroom. Brush with melted butter and roll each skewer in the breadcrumbs; cook on the grill over hot coals for 20–25 minutes, basting with butter and turning frequently. Sprinkle with chopped parsley and serve with lemon wedges.

Minted Lamb Brochettes with Apricot

Serves 8

1½ kilos/3lbs lamb, cut from the leg
  or shoulder
salt and pepper
75g/3oz plain flour
3 eggs
juice of 2 lemons
75g/3oz cornflakes
10ml/2 teaspoons chopped mint
75g/3oz fresh breadcrumbs
425g/15oz can apricot halves
watercress

Cut the lamb into 2.5cm/1in cubes. Mix together the salt, pepper and flour; beat together the eggs and lemon juice. Crush the cornflakes and mix with the mint and breadcrumbs. Coat the lamb with the seasoned flour, then dip into the egg and toss in the crumb mixture. Shake off surplus crumbs. Put the meat on to skewers and cook on the grill over hot coals for 15–18 minutes, turning frequently during cooking. Drain the apricots. Serve the brochettes garnished with the apricots and watercress.

Chicken Brochettes with Prunes

Serves 8

24 prunes
24 stuffed olives
16 chicken drumsticks
30ml/2 tablespoons flour
2.5ml/½ teaspoon ground ginger
50g/2oz butter
4 oranges
see page 47 lemon barbecue baste

Soak the prunes overnight. Cook in the water for 15 minutes then drain and remove the stones. Place a stuffed olive in the cavity and press the prune together. Cut each drumstick in half. Mix together the flour and ginger in a plastic bag. Add the chicken pieces and toss to coat them with the mixture. Melt the butter in a frying pan, add the chicken and cook for 8–10 minutes, turning several times during cooking. Cut each orange into 8 wedges. Arrange the chicken, prunes and oranges on skewers, brush with the baste and cook on the grill over medium coals for 15–25 minutes, turning and basting.

Philipino Kabobs

Serves 8

1 kilo/2lbs lamb, cut from the leg or
  shoulder
425g/15oz can pineapple chunks
2 cloves garlic, crushed
45ml/3 tablespoons soy sauce
50g/2oz butter, melted

Cut the lamb into 4cm/1½in cubes and put into a shallow dish. Drain the juice from the can of pineapple; mix the juice, garlic and soy sauce together, pour over the lamb and leave to marinate for 2 hours, turning the meat during this time. Arrange the meat and pineapple on 8 skewers, brush with melted butter and cook on the grill over hot coals for 12–15 minutes, turning and basting frequently.

Oriental Kabobs
Serves 8

250ml/½ pint dry white wine
juice of 1 lemon
125ml/¼ pint oil
2 cloves garlic, crushed
5ml/1 teaspoon dried rosemary or
  sprigs of fresh rosemary
salt and pepper
450g/1lb sweetbreads
5ml/1 teaspoon salt
750g/1½lbs lamb, cut from the leg or
  shoulder
16 button mushrooms
16 very small tomatoes

Mix together the wine, lemon juice, oil, garlic, rosemary, salt and pepper. Wash the sweetbreads in cold water, then soak them in cold water for 1–2 hours, changing the water several times. Drain. Put the sweetbreads and 5ml/1 teaspoon of salt into a saucepan, cover with cold water, bring to the boil and simmer for 15 minutes. Drain and refresh under cold water. Cut away as much white membrane as possible then cut the sweetbreads into 2.5cm/1in pieces. Cut the lamb into 2.5cm/1in pieces. Put the sweetbreads and lamb into a shallow dish, pour over the wine marinade and leave for 4 hours. Arrange the sweetbreads, lamb, mushrooms and tomatoes on skewers. Brush well with the marinade and cook on the grill over hot coals for 12–15 minutes, turning and basting frequently. Serve with oregano butter, see page 102.

Seekh Kabobs
Serves 8

1 kilo/2lbs minced raw lamb
50g/2oz fresh white breadcrumbs
100g/4oz onion, peeled and finely
  chopped
25g/1oz flour
10ml/2 teaspoons salt
2 cloves garlic, crushed
5ml/1 teaspoon ground cinnamon
5ml/1 teaspoon ground cloves
2.5ml/½ teaspoon chilli powder
finely grated rind and juice of 1
  lemon
ground black pepper
125ml/5fl. oz yogurt
chopped parsley
Savoury rice

Mix all the ingredients together, except yogurt, parsley and rice. Turn the mixture on to a well-floured board and knead lightly. Divide the mixture into 16 pieces and shape each into a sausage, about 10cm/4in long. Thread 2 kabobs lengthwise on to 8 skewers and cook over medium coals for 8–10 minutes, turning frequently until the kabobs are cooked and a golden brown. Put the savoury rice on a serving dish, arrange the kabobs on top, spoon over the yogurt and sprinkle with parsley.

Scallop Kabobs
Serves 8

24 scallops
125ml/¼ pint oil
125ml/¼ pint white wine
25g/1oz chopped onion
2 cloves garlic, crushed
30ml/2 tablespoons chopped parsley
salt and pepper
8 rashers streaky bacon
24 button mushrooms

Wash the scallops and cut each in half. Put them into a shallow dish. Mix together the oil, wine, onion, garlic, parsley, salt and pepper and pour over the scallops. Leave in the refrigerator for 3–4 hours, turning the scallops occasionally. Remove the rind from the bacon, cut each rasher in half and stretch with a knife, make into bacon rolls. Assemble the scallops, bacon and mushrooms on the skewers, brush with the marinade and cook on the grill over hot coals for 8–10 minutes, turning frequently and basting with the marinade.

South American Anticuchos
Serves 8

1½ kilos/3lbs beef heart
10ml/1 dessertspoon salt
10ml/1 dessertspoon chilli powder
ground black pepper
2 cloves garlic, crushed
125ml/¼ pint red wine
125ml/¼ pint vinegar
250ml/½ pint oil
2 green peppers
2 red peppers
24 small onions

Remove all the fat from the heart, cut into 2.5cm/1in cubes and put into a dish. Mix together the salt, chilli powder, pepper, garlic, red wine, vinegar and oil. Pour over the heart and leave covered in the refrigerator to marinate overnight. When ready to cook, drain the heart but reserve the marinade. Cut the peppers in half, remove the seeds and cut the flesh into 2.5cm/1in pieces. Peel the onions. Thread the heart, peppers and onions on to skewers, brush with the marinade and cook on the grill over hot coals for 12–15 minutes, turning and basting with the marinade during cooking. Do not overcook.

Savoury Rice
Serves 8

150g/6oz long grain rice
50g/2oz butter
100g/4oz onion, chopped
150g/6oz smoked sausage
100g/4oz cooked peas
2 tomatoes
salt and pepper
2.5ml/½ teaspoon oregano

Cook the rice in boiling salted water for 15 minutes, drain well. Melt the butter in a frying pan, add the onion and cook for 5 minutes. Cut the sausage into 1.25cm/½in slices, add to the onion and cook 3–4 minutes. Stir in the rice and peas. Skin, remove the seeds and chop the tomatoes. Add to the tomatoes with a knob of butter and heat a further 5 minutes. This mixture can be kept hot on the side of the grill.

Poultry

Small chickens and ducklings can be cut down the backbone and opened out for cooking on the grill; chicken, duck and turkey portions of varying sizes barbecue well too.

Marinate poultry well before cooking and baste well with the marinade or another baste during cooking.

Always start cooking poultry with the cut or bony side down towards the coals; the bone helps to act as a heat conductor. If no marinade is used brush well with melted butter during cooking.

Ducks tend to be fatter than other poultry so before barbecuing prick the skin well with a fork to release the fat; place the drip pan underneath the duck to catch the drippings.

Chinese Duckling

Serves 8

2–4 ducklings
salt and pepper
3 egg yolks
45ml/3 tablespoons soy sauce
30ml/2 tablespoons clear honey

Halve or quarter the ducklings, prick the skin and sprinkle with salt and pepper. Mix together the egg yolks, soy sauce and honey and rub this mixture well into the ducklings. Put them on the grill and cook over low coals, cut side down, for 45–60 minutes, turning and basting with the 'drippings' from the ducklings several times during cooking. Serve with an orange salad.

Paprika Barbecued Chicken

Serves 8

8 chicken portions
250ml/½ pint oil
3 cloves garlic, crushed
100g/4oz onion, chopped
salt and pepper
90ml/6 tablespoons paprika pepper

Wash and dry the chicken and put into a shallow dish. Mix together all the other ingredients and pour over the chicken; leave to marinate for 3–4 hours, turning the chicken several times. Drain the chicken, put on the grill and cook over hot coals for 30–35 minutes, turning frequently and basting with the marinade.

Golden Pheasant Barbecue
Serves 8

2–4 pheasants
125ml/¼ pint clear honey
10ml/2 teaspoons made mustard
30ml/2 tablespoons Worcestershire
 sauce
125ml/¼ pint wine vinegar
few drops Tabasco
285g/10½oz can mandarin oranges
125ml/¼ pint red wine
100g/4oz butter, melted
salt and pepper

Split the pheasants in half if using 4 birds, or into quarters if using 2, and put the pheasants in a shallow dish. Mix together the honey, mustard, Worcestershire sauce, wine vinegar, Tabasco, the juice from the can of oranges and red wine. Pour over the pheasants, cover and leave to marinate for 6–8 hours in the refrigerator. Drain and brush the pheasants with the melted butter, season with salt and pepper and cook on the grill, cut side down, over hot coals for 30–40 minutes, depending on the size of the pheasants. During cooking, turn and baste frequently with melted butter. Serve the pheasants with mandarin oranges and garnish with watercress.

Golden Crisp Duck
Serves 8

8 duck portions
100g/4oz dried breadcrumbs
salt and pepper
grated rind of 1 orange
2 eggs
65ml/2½fl. oz orange juice
8 orange wedges
watercress

Remove the skin from the duck, wash and dry well. In a plastic bag mix together the crumbs, salt, pepper and orange rind. In a dish beat together the eggs and orange juice. Coat the duck with the egg mixture, then put the portions, one at a time, in the bag and coat well with the crumbs. Remove the portion from the bag and shake well to remove surplus crumbs. Put the duck on the grill and cook over medium coals for 35–40 minutes, turning occasionally, until the duck is cooked and a golden brown. Serve with watercress and orange wedges.

Ranch Style Chicken
Serves 8

125ml/¼ pint apple juice
45ml/3 tablespoons oil
10ml/2 teaspoons Worcestershire
 sauce
25g/1oz onion, chopped
1 clove garlic, crushed
salt and pepper
5ml/1 teaspoon paprika pepper
10ml/2 teaspoons tomato paste
few drops Tabasco
2.5ml/½ teaspoon dry mustard
8 chicken portions
50g/2oz butter, melted

Put all the ingredients, except chicken and butter, into a screw top jar, cover and shake well. Put the chicken in a dish, pour over the mixture and leave in the refrigerator to marinate for 12 hours, turn the chicken twice during this time. Drain the chicken, brush with the melted butter, put on the grill and cook over hot coals for 30–35 minutes, turning and basting with melted butter several times during cooking.

Kebabs with olives (p. 61)

Cream cheese and olive
dip (p. 42)

A good selection of drinks helps
get your guests in the party mood

Sugar baby party bowl (p. 97)

Brandied Smoked Chicken
Serves 8

4 small chickens
chicken seasoning
100g/4oz butter
60ml/4 tablespoons brandy
50g/2oz Demerara sugar
juice of 2 lemons
210g/7½oz can red cherries
210g/7½oz can apricot halves

Split the chickens in half lengthwise, wash and dry, and sprinkle with the chicken seasoning. Heat together in a small saucepan the butter, brandy, sugar and lemon juice. Empty the cans of cherries and apricots into a small saucepan. Brush the chickens with the brandy baste, put the chickens on the grill and cook over hot coals for 30–40 minutes. Baste frequently with the brandy mixture and turn the chickens several times during cooking. During the last 10 minutes of the cooking time add a few pieces of damp apple wood to the coals; this will give a smokey flavour to the chicken. Some time before the chicken is cooked put the saucepan containing the fruit on the grill to heat through. Serve the chicken with the fruit on top as a garnish.

Barbecued Chicken Drumsticks
Serves 8

8 chicken drumsticks
50g/2oz butter
50g/2oz onion, chopped
210g/7½oz can tomatoes
30ml/2 tablespoons Worcestershire
  sauce
25g/1oz Demerara sugar
salt and pepper

Trim off any excess skin from the chicken. Melt the butter in a saucepan, add the onion and fry for 2–3 minutes. Add the tomatoes, Worcestershire sauce, sugar and salt and pepper, simmer for 10 minutes. Rub through a sieve or liquidize. Brush the drumsticks with the sauce, put on the grill and cook over hot coals for 20–25 minutes, turning and basting with the tomato sauce several times during cooking. Serve the chicken with the remainder of the sauce separately.

Mixed Herb Turkey
Serves 8

250ml/½ pint sherry
125ml/¼ pint oil
50g/2oz onion, chopped
15ml/1 tablespoon Worcestershire
  sauce
juice of 1 lemon
1 clove garlic, crushed
5ml/1 teaspoon thyme
5ml/1 teaspoon oregano
5ml/1 teaspoon rosemary
5ml/1 teaspoon marjoram
salt and pepper
8 turkey drumsticks

Mix together all the ingredients, except the turkey, in a screw top jar and shake well, leave for 4 hours so that the flavours blend. Put the turkey in a dish, pour over the mixture and leave to marinate for 2 hours. Drain the turkey, put on the grill and cook over medium coals for 1–1¼ hours, turning and basting with the marinade several times during cooking.

Mandarin Chicken Bundles

Serves 8

3 carrots
8 chicken portions
salt and pepper
285g/10oz can mandarin oranges
juice of 2 lemons
8 sprigs of rosemary
15ml/1 tablespoon cornflour
250ml/$\frac{1}{2}$ pint chicken stock
chopped parsley

Peel and cut the carrots into thin sticks. Wash and dry the chicken, season with salt and pepper and place each on a square of double thickness foil. Drain the juice from the oranges, reserving the juice and a few oranges for the sauce. Divide the remaining oranges and carrot sticks between the chicken. Sprinkle over the lemon juice and add a sprig of rosemary to each piece of chicken. Gather the foil up to make a bundle and put in the coals to cook for 35–40 minutes. Meanwhile make up the sauce. Put the cornflour in a small saucepan, blend in the stock and mandarin juice, bring to the boil, stirring all the time, and simmer for 2–3 minutes. Add the remaining oranges and chopped parsley. To serve, open the bundles, glaze the chicken with a little sauce and serve the rest separately.

Lemon Grilled Chicken

Serves 8

4 young chickens, about 1 kilo/2lbs each
2 lemons
75g/3oz butter, melted
salt and ground black pepper
paprika pepper

Wipe the chickens and split in half lengthwise. Cut the lemons in half and rub all sides of the chicken with the lemon, squeezing the juice over the flesh. Place the chicken in a dish, cover and refrigerate for 3 hours. Brush the chicken with the melted butter, sprinkle with salt and pepper and put them on the grill. Cook over hot coals for 25–30 minutes, turning and brushing several times with melted butter during cooking. Test the chicken with a skewer to see if it is cooked, the juices should run clear.

Eastern Ginger Chicken

Serves 8

8 chicken portions
125ml/$\frac{1}{4}$ pint oil
125ml/$\frac{1}{4}$ pint white wine
15ml/1 tablespoon wine vinegar
1 clove garlic, crushed
100g/4oz onion, chopped
15ml/1 tablespoon French mustard
5ml/1 teaspoon ground ginger
30ml/2 tablespoons soy sauce
10ml/2 teaspoons chilli sauce
juice of 2 lemons

Wash and put the chicken portions in a shallow dish. Mix all the other ingredients together and pour over the chicken. Cover and marinate in the refrigerator for 4–6 hours, turning the chicken several times. Place the chicken on the grill and cook over hot coals for 30–40 minutes, basting with the marinade and turning the chicken several times during cooking.

Sesame Chicken Breasts
Serves 8

8 chicken breasts
salt and pepper
125ml/¼ pint soy sauce
125ml/¼ pint dry sherry
125ml/¼ pint oil
2.5ml/½ teaspoon ground ginger
25g/1oz toasted sesame seeds

Put the chicken into a shallow dish. Mix together all the other ingredients, except the sesame seeds, and pour over the chicken. Leave to marinate for 1–2 hours. Drain the chicken and cook on the grill over hot coals for 25–30 minutes, turning and basting with the marinade during cooking. Sprinkle with the sesame seeds before serving.

Spicy Spanish Chicken
Serves 8

8 chicken portions
200g/8oz butter, melted
2 cloves garlic, crushed
salt and pepper
10ml/2 teaspoons paprika pepper
2.5ml/½ teaspoon ground cinnamon
2.5ml/½ teaspoon crushed tarragon

Wash and dry the chicken. Put all the other ingredients together in a small saucepan and heat for a few minutes. Brush the chicken with the sauce and cook on the grill over hot coals for 30–35 minutes, turning occasionally and basting frequently with the butter sauce. Serve with Savoury Rice, see page 66.

Crispy Chicken Pieces
Serves 8

8 large chicken breasts
100g/4oz plain flour
200g/8oz butter, melted
salt and pepper

Wash and dry the chicken. Mix together in a plastic bag the flour, salt and pepper. Dip the chicken into melted butter and then put them, one at a time, in the bag and coat thoroughly with the flour. Put the chicken on the grill and cook over hot coals for 8–10 minutes on each side, turning once and basting well during cooking with the melted butter.

Californian Barbecued Chicken
Serves 8

8 chicken portions
juice of 2 lemons
100g/4oz butter, melted
salt
ground black pepper
Californian barbecue baste, see page 46

Wash and dry the chicken portions. Mix together the lemon juice, melted butter, salt and pepper; brush the chicken with this baste and cook on the grill over medium coals for 35–40 minutes. During cooking turn the chicken and baste with the barbecue baste frequently.

Meat

GENERAL HINTS ON PREPARING MEATS FOR THE BARBECUE

1. Allow meat to come to room temperature before cooking, it will then absorb flavours from bastes and sauces better. As a guide:
   Chicken portions require about 30 minutes
   Steaks and chops require about 1–2 hours
   Joints and whole chickens require about 2–3 hours.
2. Trim off excess fat from the meat where necessary, then score the remaining fat on steaks, chops, ham to prevent the outer edges from curling during cooking.
3. Rub the barbecue grill well with a piece of fat on a fork to prevent food from sticking.
4. Prepare marinades, bastes and sauces well in advance.
5. Season the meat with salt and pepper.
6. Turn foods such as hamburgers, steaks, chops and gammon to achieve a lattice pattern from the grill on which they are cooked.
7. Both surfaces of the meat should be seared quickly to seal in the juices.
8. Do not poke food with a fork, this will cause the juices to run, always turn with tongs.
9. Do not crowd the grill for this will give an excess of smoke and allow a 7.5cm/3in gap between the charcoal and the grill.
10. Gammon steaks or large flat pieces of meat which are likely to curl during cooking can be kept flat by piercing through the meat horizontally with a skewer.

BEEF

The delicious smell of barbecued steaks, what could be better? Select good quality meat and have the steaks, fillet, rump, porterhouse and sirloin about 2–2.5cm/$\frac{3}{4}$–1in thick. They can be cooked fairly close to the fire for rare steaks to several inches above the coals for steaks that are well-done. If flank steak is to be served it must only be cooked rare otherwise it will be tough. Steaks can be marinated to tenderize, the longer they are left in the marinade the stronger the flavour will be. Alternatively just rub with a clove of garlic and brush with melted butter before cooking. For a small party cook a large steak, then slice for serving.

Surprise Steak Turnover
Serves 8

400g/1lb shortcrust pastry
8 sirloin steaks, about 2.5cm/1in
  thick by 8cm by 10cm/3in by 4in
oil
salt
garlic
ground black pepper

Divide the pastry into 8 portions and roll each out into a circle. Brush each steak with oil and season with garlic salt and pepper. Place a steak on to each round of pastry, moisten the edges, fold the pastry over and seal well. Prick the pastry several times with a fork. Cook the turnovers on the grill over low coals for about 35–45 minutes, turning them several times during cooking. With care during cooking the crust need not be too charred so that the whole turnover can be eaten, but if it is too brown then the steak inside will still be quite delicious.

Beef Tenderloin Vermouth
Serves 8–12

1$\frac{1}{2}$–2 kilos/3–4lbs beef tenderloin
125ml/$\frac{1}{4}$ pint oil
250ml/$\frac{1}{2}$ pint red wine
125ml/$\frac{1}{4}$ pint lemon juice
2 cloves garlic, crushed
2 bay leaves
salt and pepper
30ml/2 tablespoons dry vermouth

Wipe and trim the tenderloin and place in a strong plastic bag. Mix together all the other ingredients, except the vermouth, and pour into the bag. Tie the bag securely and tip to coat the meat with the liquid. Place the bag in a bowl and leave in the refrigerator for 12–24 hours, turning the bag over several times. Drain the meat and cook on the grill over hot coals for 30–50 minutes, turning and basting with the marinade. Place the meat on a board, sprinkle with the vermouth and cut into slices for serving.

Périgord Steak

Serves 8

8 steaks
salt and pepper
65ml/2½fl. oz oil
200g/8oz pâté de foie gras
125ml/¼ pint sherry

Season the steaks with salt and pepper, brush with oil and grill over hot coals for 12–25 minutes, turning once or twice during cooking. Meanwhile mix together the pâté and sherry and, just before serving the steaks, spread each with some of the pâté mixture. Complete the cooking time and serve the steaks.

Steak aux Champignons

Serves 8

3 large onions
200g/8oz mushrooms
50g/2oz butter
2 cloves garlic, crushed
salt and pepper
8 porterhouse steaks, 5cm/2in thick
65ml/2½fl. oz soy sauce
125ml/¼ pint red wine

Peel and finely chop the onions, wash and thinly slice the mushrooms. Melt the butter, add the onions and mushrooms and fry 3–4 minutes. Add the garlic, salt and pepper and cook a further 2–3 minutes. Cut a horizontal slit, on one side, through the centre of each steak to form a 'pocket'. Do not cut right through the steak. Fill each 'pocket' with the mushroom mixture. Mix together the soy sauce and wine and brush over the steaks. Cook on the grill over hot coals for 12–15 minutes. Turn once and brush with the sauce during cooking.

Steak au Poivre

Serves 8

25g/1oz black pepper corns
8 steaks
4 large tomatoes
50g/2oz butter, melted
15ml/1 tablespoon basil
salt
65ml/2½fl. oz. brandy

Crush the pepper corns and rub into both sides of the steaks. Leave to stand at room temperature for 30 minutes. Cook on the grill over hot coals for 10–20 minutes, turning once or twice during cooking. Meanwhile cut the tomatoes in half, brush with the melted butter and sprinkle with basil and salt and cook on the grill for 5–6 minutes. Place the steaks on a serving dish with half a tomato on each. Warm the brandy, ignite and spoon over the steaks.

Flank Steak Teriyaki

Serves 8

2 kilos/4lbs flank steak
125ml/¼ pint soy sauce
250ml/½ pint red wine
125ml/¼ pint oil
2 cloves garlic, crushed
salt and pepper

Beat the steak well with steak hammer or rolling pin. Put the steak in a dish. Mix together all the other ingredients and pour over the steak. Leave in the refrigerator to marinate for at least 12 hours, turning once or twice during this time. Place the steak on the grill and cook over hot coals for 3–5 minutes on each side. Flank steak should only be served rare. Garnish with savoury butter and watercress.

Steak à la crème
Serves 8

250ml/½ pint soured cream
finely grated rind and juice of 2
  lemons
125ml/¼ pint oil
2 cloves garlic, crushed
30ml/2 tablespoons Worcestershire
  sauce
5ml/1 teaspoon paprika pepper
5ml/1 teaspoon marjoram
salt and pepper
8 steaks

Mix all the ingredients together, except steaks, in a screw top jar and shake well. Place the steaks in a shallow dish, pour over the mixture and leave to marinate for 3–4 hours. Place the steaks on the grill and cook over hot coals for 12–15 minutes, turning and basting with the marinade. Sprinkle the steaks with ground black pepper before serving.

Simple Grilled Steak
Serves 8

8 steaks
salt and pepper
parsley butter, see page 102
watercress

Place the steaks on the grill, sprinkle with salt and pepper, and cook over hot coals for 12–25 minutes, turning once. Place the steaks on a serving dish and top with parsley butter and garnish with watercress.

Steak Provençale
Serves 8

200g/8 oz shallots
30ml/2 tablespoons oil
400g/1lb tomatoes
2 cloves garlic, crushed
salt and pepper
5ml/1 teaspoon basil
15ml/1 tablespoon chopped parsley
8 steaks

Peel and chop the shallots. Heat the oil and fry them for 4–5 minutes until soft. Skin and chop the tomatoes and add to the frying pan with the garlic, salt, pepper and basil. Cook a further 3–4 minutes then stir in the parsley. Season the steaks, brush with oil and cook over hot coals for 12–15 minutes, turning once or twice during cooking. Place the steaks on a serving dish and pile the tomato mixture on each one.

Roquefort Steak
Serves 8

8 steaks
salt and pepper
200g/8oz Roquefort cheese
125ml/¼ pint oil
3 cloves garlic, crushed
40ml/4 tablespoons red wine

Season the steaks with salt and pepper and cook on the grill over hot coals for 12–25 minutes, turning once. Mix together the cheese, oil, garlic and wine. A few minutes before the steaks are completely cooked spread some of the cheese mixture on each one and complete the cooking time.

PORK

Lots of cuts to choose from – chump, loin and spare rib chops, belly slices and spare ribs are all good cuts to cook on the barbecue. Pork cut from the leg or fillet is excellent meat to use in skewer cooking. Trim off excess fat before cooking. Pork should always be well cooked.

Spiced Lemon Chops
Serves 8

8 spare rib pork chops
125ml/¼ pint oil
45ml/3 tablespoons lemon juice
5ml/1 teaspoon nutmeg
5ml/1 teaspoon sage
15ml/1 tablespoon brown sugar

Trim excess fat from the chops and put into a shallow dish. Mix together all the other ingredients and pour over the chops. Leave to marinate for 2–3 hours. Drain the chops, put on the grill and cook over medium coals for 25–30 minutes, turning and basting with the mixture several times during cooking.

Coated Belly Slices
Serves 8

8 slices belly pork
beaten egg
sage and onion stuffing
8 × 2.5cm/1in slices of cooking apple
25g/1oz Demerara sugar

Remove the rind from the pork. Dip each slice of pork into the beaten egg then coat well with dry sage and onion stuffing. Put the slices on to a well-greased grill and cook over medium coals for 20–25 minutes, turning twice during cooking. During the last 10 minutes of the cooking time place an apple slice on each piece of pork, sprinkle with Demerara sugar and complete the cooking time.

Cream Pork Fillet
Serves 8

125ml/¼ pint soy sauce
65ml/2½fl. oz dry sherry
5ml/1 teaspoon made mustard
salt and pepper
1 kilo/2lbs pork fillet
300g/12oz mushrooms
50g/2oz butter
125ml/5fl. oz soured cream
1.25ml/¼ teaspoon dill weed
salt and pepper
paprika pepper
chopped parsley

Mix together in a basin the soy sauce, sherry, mustard, salt and pepper. Cut the fillets in half lengthwise, remove surplus fat and sinews, and flatten the meat with a hammer or rolling pin. Brush the meat with the sherry mixture, put them on the grill and cook over medium coals for 15–20 minutes, turning and basting frequently. Meanwhile, wash and slice the mushrooms, melt the butter, add the mushrooms and fry for 5–6 minutes. Stir in the soured cream, dill weed and salt and pepper to taste. Cut the pork into slices, arrange on a serving dish and pour the sauce down the centre. Sprinkle with paprika pepper and chopped parsley.

Stuffed Pork Steaks
Serves 8

75g/3oz shallots
200g/8oz chicken livers
50g/2oz butter
100g/4oz mushrooms
25g/1oz fresh white breadcrumbs
2.5ml/½ teaspoon dill weed
salt and pepper
8 pork steaks
30ml/2 tablespoons oil
chopped parsley

Peel and finely chop the shallots. Chop the livers. Melt the butter in a frying pan, add the shallots and livers and fry 2–3 minutes. Wash and chop the mushrooms, add to the frying pan and cook a further 4–5 minutes. Stir in the breadcrumbs, dill weed and seasoning to taste. Cut a pocket in each steak and fill with the mixture. Brush the steaks with a little oil, put on the grill and cook over medium coals for 20–30 minutes, turning and brushing with more oil several times during cooking. Serve the steaks sprinkled with chopped parsley.

Gammon Steaks with Seville Sauce
Serves 8

8 gammon steaks
30ml/2 tablespoons oil
60ml/4 tablespoons Worcestershire
  sauce
grated rind and juice of 2 oranges
salt and pepper
15ml/1 tablespoon cornflour
250ml/½ pint water
150g/6oz chunky marmalade

Score the fat on the gammon to prevent curling during cooking and put into a shallow dish. Mix together the oil, Worcestershire sauce, rind and juice of the oranges, salt and pepper and pour over the gammon. Leave to marinate for 2 hours, turning occasionally. Remove the gammon, reserving the marinade, and cook the gammon on the grill over medium coals for 20–30 minutes, turning once and brushing with the marinade. Meanwhile put the cornflour in a small saucepan, blend in the water, add any remaining marinade and the marmalade. Bring to the boil, stirring all the time and simmer for 2–3 minutes. Arrange the gammon on a serving dish and pour the sauce over.

Sharp Spare Rib Chops
Serves 8

285g/10oz can pineapple slices
100g/4oz Demerara sugar
10ml/1 dessertspoon French mustard
8 spare rib pork chops
watercress

Drain the juice from the can of pineapple. Mix together 30ml/2 tablespoons pineapple juice, sugar and mustard. Slash the fat on the chops and brush one side with the sugar mixture, put this side down on the greased grill and cook over medium coals for 20–30 minutes, turning and basting once with the sauce. Put a slice of pineapple on each chop and leave to cook a further 2–3 minutes. Serve the chops garnished with watercress.

Cranberry Barbecued Chops

Serves 8

8 pork chops
salt and pepper
184g/6½oz jar cranberry sauce
6oml/3 tablespoons clear honey
2.5ml/½ teaspoon ground cloves
2.5ml/½ teaspoon nutmeg

Snip the fat on the chops and sprinkle with salt and pepper. Mix together all the other ingredients and brush over the chops. Put the chops on the grill and cook over medium coals for 25–30 minutes, turning and basting with the sauce. Arrange the chops on a serving dish, pour over any remaining sauce and sprinkle with chopped parsley.

Chopped Ham with Peaches

Serves 8

425g/15oz can peach slices
184g/6½oz jar cranberry sauce
2.5ml/½ teaspoon ground ginger
3oml/2 tablespoons lemon juice
2 × 340g/12oz can chopped ham and pork

Drain the juice from the can of peaches. In a small saucepan mix together the juice, cranberry sauce and ginger. Heat and simmer for 2–3 minutes, add the lemon juice and peach slices, leave on the side of the grill to keep warm. Cut the meat into slices, brush with the sauce and cook on the grill over hot coals for 10–15 minutes, turning and basting with the sauce during cooking. Arrange the meat on a serving dish and pour the sauce and peaches over.

Ham and Pineapple Slice

Serves 8

285g/10oz can pineapple slices
25g/1oz brown sugar
5ml/1 teaspoon made mustard
3oml/2 tablespoons vinegar
8 portions cooked ham, 1.25cm/½in thick
cooked rice
watercress

Drain the juice from the can of pineapple. In a small saucepan mix together the juice, sugar, mustard and vinegar, heat for 5 minutes. Brush the ham with the baste and cook on the grill over medium coals for 8–10 minutes, turning once and brushing with the baste. Put a pineapple slice on each piece of ham, brush with more baste and cook a further 2–3 minutes. Put the rice on a serving dish, arrange the ham on top and garnish with watercress.

Nutty Pork Chops

Serves 8

100g/4oz peanut butter
125ml/¼ pint orange juice
8 pork chops
salt and pepper
25g/1oz toasted flaked almonds
watercress and orange salad

Mix together the peanut butter and orange juice. Snip the fat on the chops and season with salt and pepper. Put the chops on the grill and cook over medium coals for 20–30 minutes, turning and basting with the orange mixture several times during cooking. Serve the chops sprinkled with the almonds and the salad.

Barbecued Spare Ribs are so delicious; you should plan to serve at least 300g/12oz per person. The ribs can be cut into portions, marinated before cooking on the grill and then during cooking the marinade can be used as a baste; this will impart a good flavour as well as giving the ribs a glaze. They will take about 35 minutes to cook if cut into 2 rib portions but up to $1\frac{1}{2}$ hours if the spare rib is left whole. The ribs can be pre-cooked by roasting in the oven or by covering with spiced water and cooking in a saucepan. Recipes in the Marinade, Bastes and Sauce section can be used for cooking with spare ribs.

To roast spare ribs before cooking on the grill.
Put the spare ribs in a shallow dish, pour over a marinade, cover and leave for up to 24 hours. Drain and put them in a roasting tin; cook at Gas 4 or 180°C/350°F for about 1 hour. When ready to barbecue put the ribs on to a well greased grill, brush with the reserved marinade and cook for 10–15 minutes, turning and basting frequently, until glazed and crisp.

To simmer spare ribs before cooking on the grill – 3 kilos/6lbs.
Put the ribs into a saucepan and cover with cold water. Add salt and pepper, a few cloves, 2 bay leaves and 2 cloves garlic. Bring to the boil then simmer for 30 minutes. Drain well and leave in the refrigerator until required. They can then be cooked on the grill for about 10–15 minutes basting with a sauce.

To cook spare ribs straight on the grill.
Cut into 2 rib portions, rub with salt and put on the grill and cook over medium coals for about 10 minutes, turning once. Then start basting with the sauce and do this for a further 25–30 minutes, turning very frequently.

LAMB

A great favourite the world over for the barbecue because it is usually tender. Loin and chump chops and cutlets are excellent to cook over the coals and for skewer cooking choose cuts from the leg or shoulder. Lamb can be cooked medium-rare with a golden brown crisp outside but still just slightly pink and moist in the inside. Breast of lamb cut into small strips, marinated to tenderize and to bring out the flavour, makes a delicious inexpensive dish for informal entertaining.

Sweet and Spicy Noisettes
Serves 8

15ml/1 tablespoon honey
10ml/1 dessertspoon dry mustard
salt and pepper
15ml/1 tablespoon lemon juice
1 clove garlic, crushed
8 noisettes of lamb, cut from the loin
425g/15oz can pineapple rings
50g/2oz butter
20ml/2 dessertspoons chopped mint

Mix together the honey, mustard, salt, pepper, lemon juice and garlic. Spread this mixture over the noisettes and leave to stand for 20 minutes. Drain the juice from the pineapple. Put 60ml/4 tablespoons pineapple juice and the butter into a small saucepan, heat to melt the butter then simmer for 5 minutes. Remove the saucepan from the heat and add the chopped mint. The saucepan should now be put on the side of the grill to keep warm. Brush the noisettes with the pineapple baste, put them on the grill and cook over medium coals for 30–35 minutes, turning and basting with the pineapple mixture several times. During the last 5 minutes of the cooking time put the pineapple rings on the grill and heat through. Serve a noisette on a pineapple ring with any remaining pineapple baste poured over.

Barbecued Chops Oriental
Serves 8

8 chump chops
1 clove garlic, crushed
125ml/¼ pint soy sauce
125ml/¼ pint water
salt and pepper

Trim the chops and place in a shallow dish. Mix together all the other ingredients and pour over the chops. Cover and leave in the refrigerator to marinate overnight. Drain the chops and put on the grill, cook over medium coals for 20–25 minutes, turning several times during cooking. Serve the chops with hot rice and chop suey.

Chops in a Parcel
Serves 8

4 eggs, hard-boiled
75g/3oz fresh white breadcrumbs
2 cloves garlic, crushed
salt and pepper
30ml/2 tablespoons chopped parsley
75g/3oz butter, melted
8 lamb loin chops

Chop the hard-boiled eggs, add the breadcrumbs, garlic, salt, pepper, chopped parsley and melted butter. Make the chops into a round and cover each chop with the mixture. Wrap each chop in a double thickness of foil and put the parcels on the grill. Cook over medium coals for 30–35 minutes. Open the parcels and serve the chops.

Mint Glazed Cutlets
Serves 8

16 lamb cutlets
salt and pepper
60ml/4 tablespoons mint jelly

Season the cutlets with salt and pepper and spread with half the mint jelly. Cook the cutlets on the grill over medium coals for 12–20 minutes, turning once and spreading with the remaining mint jelly.

Devilled Lamb Chops

Serves 8

8 New Zealand lamb chump chops
salt and pepper
30ml/2 tablespoons French mustard
200g/8oz brown sugar

Trim the chops, season with salt and pepper and spread with half the mustard and sugar. Put the chops on the grill and cook over medium coals for 5–8 minutes. Turn over and spread with more mustard and sugar, cook a further 5–8 minutes.

Spicy Barbecued Lamb

Serves 8

3–4 large breasts of lamb
250ml/½ pint cider
60ml/4 tablespoons Worcestershire
  sauce
50g/2oz Demerara sugar
60ml/4 tablespoons red wine vinegar
50g/2oz onion, finely chopped
5ml/1 teaspoon dried rosemary
salt and pepper
lemon wedges

Trim any excess fat from the lamb, cut into strips between the bones with a sharp knife and place in a dish. Mix all the other ingredients together, except lemon wedges, in a small saucepan and bring to the boil, allow to simmer for 3–4 minutes, then leave to cool. Pour the cold marinade over the lamb and leave for at least 3 hours, turning the meat occasionally. Drain the lamb and put on the grill, cook over medium coals for 12–16 minutes, turning and basting frequently until crisp and a golden brown.

Lamb Chops Parmesan

Serves 8

8 chump lamb chops
lamb marinade, see page 46
100g/4oz grated Parmesan cheese
100g/4oz butter
grated rind and juice of 1 lemon
1 clove garlic, crushed

Trim the chops, put in a dish and pour over the marinade, leave for 2–3 hours. Put the chops on the grill and cook over medium coals for 12–20 minutes, turning and basting once. Beat together the cheese, butter, lemon juice and rind and garlic. A few minutes before serving the chops top with the cheese mixture. Allow the mixture to start melting before serving.

Rosé Lamb Steaks

Serves 8

8 lamb chops, 2.5cm/1in thick, cut
  from the leg
125ml/¼ pint oil
125ml/¼ pint lemon juice
125ml/¼ pint rosé wine
2 cloves garlic, crushed
3–4 sprigs rosemary
salt and pepper
30ml/2 tablespoons chopped parsley

Trim the lamb and place in a shallow dish. Mix together all the other ingredients, pour over the meat and leave to marinate for 2 hours. Drain the meat, place on the grill and cook over medium coals for 20–25 minutes, turning and basting with the marinade frequently.

Barbecue Lamb Ribs

Serves 8

3 large breasts of lamb, cut into riblets
1½ litres/3 pints water
45ml/3 tablespoons vinegar
45ml/3 tablespoons soy sauce
45ml/3 tablespoons clear honey
45ml/3 tablespoons plum jam
30ml/3 dessertspoons white vinegar
10ml/1 dessertspoon Worcestershire sauce
10ml/1 dessertspoon dry mustard
45ml/3 tablespoons tomato ketchup
juice of 1 lemon

Remove the excess fat from the lamb. Boil the water and vinegar together, add the lamb and simmer for 15 minutes. Mix all the other ingredients together for the sauce in a small saucepan and heat slowly until blended. Drain the lamb and arrange on the grill, brush with the sauce and cook over medium coals 12–20 minutes, turning and basting with the sauce several times. Serve the ribs with any remaining sauce.

Buttered Lamb Cutlets

Serves 8

8 lamb cutlets
salt and pepper
100g/4oz butter
45ml/3 tablespoons chopped parlsey
45ml/3 tablespoons chopped mint
2 cloves garlic, crushed

Trim the cutlets, season with salt and pepper and brush with a little oil. Put the cutlets on the grill and cook over medium coals for 12–18 minutes, turning once and brushing with a little more oil. Meanwhile mix together the butter, parsley, mint and garlic; shape into a roll, wrap in foil and put in the refrigerator until required. Serve a cutlet with a round of butter on top, serve quickly.

Butterfly Lamb

Serves 8

2–2½ kilos/4–5lbs leg of lamb
1 clove garlic, crushed
salt and pepper
5ml/1 teaspoon chopped mint
50g/2oz onion, chopped
125ml/¼ pint oil
125ml/¼ pint lemon juice

Have the lamb boned and split lengthwise so that it lays flat. Mix together all the other ingredients for the marinade; put the lamb in a shallow dish, pour over the marinade, cover and leave for 4–5 hours, turning occasionally. Drain and reserve the liquid. Place two long skewers through the lamb at right angles to form an X to keep the lamb flat during cooking, or place the lamb in a hinged grill basket. Cook the lamb on the grill over medium coals for 1½–2 hours, turning and basting frequently. When cooked place the lamb on a board and slice thinly.

Spit cooking

Spit-cooking is one of the delights of barbecuing.

Large pieces of meat and poultry cooked in this way are a joy to serve at a party. As the meat turns on the spit, its own juices and any baste used roll round with it and so the meat stays moist and full of flavour.

The meat should be deliciously crisp and a golden brown when cooked.

Brush the meat generously with a baste or sauce during cooking. Make sure the drip pan is placed underneath the food in order to catch the drippings.

If more than one piece of meat is to be cooked on the same spit do not place them too closely together so that the heat can cook all surfaces. Do make sure the meat is evenly balanced on the spit otherwise the turning will be jerky and this will result in uneven cooking.

When spit-cooking poultry make the bird as compact as possible with the wings and drumsticks close to the body. Do not put too much stuffing in the bird, as the stuffing swells during cooking it may tend to burst out. Better to put some stuffing in the cavity and use more to make stuffing balls. These can be wrapped in foil and cooked in the coals.

Herb Roasted Turkey
Serves 8–12

$2\frac{1}{2}$–3 kilos/5–6lbs turkey
salt and pepper
5 shallots
sprigs of parsley
sprigs of thyme
75g/3oz butter

Wash and dry the turkey. Sprinkle the inside with salt and pepper. Peel and slice the shallots and put with the parsley and thyme inside the turkey. Rub the skin of the turkey with the butter and sprinkle with salt and pepper. Fasten the turkey on to the spit securely and cook over low – medium coals for $1\frac{1}{2}$–2 hours.

Pleated Pork Ribs

Serves 8

60ml/4 tablespoons oil
4 onions, peeled and chopped
285g/10oz can tomato soup
50g/2oz Demerara sugar
65ml/2½fl. oz vinegar
125ml/¼ pint orange juice
salt and pepper
3–4 kilos/6–8lbs pork spare ribs

Heat the oil in a saucepan, add the chopped onions and fry for 3–4 minutes. Add all the other ingredients, except the spare ribs, and simmer for 10 minutes. Sprinkle the spare ribs with salt and pepper and pleat the ribs on to the spit, putting the spit through the fleshy part after every 4th or 5th rib. Brush the ribs well with the sauce. Arrange the hot coals either at the back of the fire-box or in 2 rows, but always having the drip pan under the meat. Allow the ribs to rotate over low coals for 1–1½ hours. Every ½ hour brush the ribs with more sauce. During the last ½ hour of cooking add a few twigs of dampened apple wood.

Royal Rib Roast

Serves 8–12

2–3 kilos/4½–6½lbs rib of beef, boned and rolled
250ml/½ pint red wine
30ml/2 tablespoons tomato ketchup
125ml/¼ pint wine vinegar
125ml/¼ pint oil
30ml/2 tablespoons Worcestershire sauce
75g/3oz onion, chopped
salt and ground black pepper
5ml/1 teaspoon rosemary

Wipe the meat and place in a large plastic bag. Mix all the other ingredients together, pour into the bag and tie securely. Put the bag in a bowl and place in the refrigerator, leave to marinate for 8–12 hours. Turn the bag several times during this period. Drain the meat, secure it on the spit and cook over medium coals for 1½–1¾ hours, basting occasionally with the marinade. Remove the meat from the spit, place on a board and slice thinly.

Honeyed Ducks

Serves 8

2 ducks
salt and pepper
125ml/¼ pint soy sauce
100g/4oz honey
orange segments
watercress

Wash and dry the ducks, prick the skin all over and sprinkle the inside with salt and pepper. Mix together the soy sauce and honey and rub some well into the skin of the ducks. Place the ducks firmly on the spit with either the coals on both sides of the fire box with the drip tray in the centre under the ducks, or the coals on one side only of the fire box, and the drip tray under the ducks. Cook over low – medium coals for 1¼–1¾ hours. Brush several times during cooking with the honey baste. For a crisper skin, place the spit nearer to the coals for the last 10 minutes of the cooking time. Cut the ducks into portions and serve each decorated with orange segments and watercress.

Lamburgers with pineapple (p. 59), beefburgers and tuna fishburgers (p. 57)

Mixed barbecue lamb grill (pp. 82–84)

Rosemary Spit Lamb

Serves 8

$2\frac{1}{2}$–3 kilos/5–7lbs leg of lamb
sprigs of rosemary
salt and pepper
100g/4oz butter, melted

Bone and roll the lamb. Put the rosemary on the outside of the lamb and tie the roll securely. Rub with salt and pepper. Secure the lamb on the spit, brush with melted butter and cook over medium .coals for $2\frac{1}{2}$–3 hours, basting with more butter during cooking. A meat thermometer should read 65°–70°C/150°–160°F. Remove the lamb from the spit, place on a board and slice thinly.

Tangy Lemon Chicken

Serves 8

2 chickens
salt and pepper
2 packets parsley and thyme stuffing
grated rind and juice of 2 lemons
5ml/1 teaspoon made mustard
100g/4oz butter, melted

Wash and dry the chickens and sprinkle the inside with salt and pepper. Make up the stuffing according to the directions on the packet and use to stuff the chickens. Fasten the neck skin to the back with a skewer and tie the wings and legs to the body. Place the chickens on the spit. Mix together the lemon juice, rind, mustard and butter, brush over the surface of the chicken. Put the coals in 2 rows on either side of the fire box with the drip pan in the centre under the chickens. Rotate the spit and cook over medium coals for $1\frac{3}{4}$–$2\frac{1}{4}$ hours.

Suckling Pig

Serves 14–16

1 pig weighing 7–8 kilos/15–18lbs
sage and onion stuffing
red apple

Ask the butcher to clean and prepare the pig for you. Stuff the pig with the stuffing and sew up with strong string. Do not overstuff the pig as the stuffing will swell during cooking. Place a piece of wood in the mouth, this is removed after cooking and replaced with the apple. Tuck the legs under the body and tie with string. Place the pig on the spit, over a deep bed of coals. The coals should be arranged in two rows with a long drip pan down the centre under the pig. Cook for 6–8 hours, basting frequently with the dripping from the pig. If the ears and nose brown too quickly cover these with foil.

For serving: Remove the pig from the spit and place on a large board; remove the piece of wood from the mouth, replace it with the apple and flowers or cherries in the eye sockets. Serve with foil-baked potatoes, apple sauce and watercress and orange salad.

Salads

For crispness and goodness, a mixed green salad is the hardy perennial to serve with barbecued food; but you will find many delicious salads in this section to tempt you to serve something just a little different. Try to have a good contrast in colour and texture in salads so that the whole meal is attractive and appetizing. Most salad foods can be prepared well in advance but only add the dressing and toss just before serving.

Avocado and Artichoke Salad
Serves 8

4 ripe avocados
juice of 2 lemons
425g/15oz can artichoke hearts
200g/8oz tomatoes
125ml/¼ pint French dressing
salt and pepper
150g/6oz cooked rice
black olives

Peel and cut the avocados in half, remove the stone and slice the flesh thinly. Sprinkle with the lemon juice. Drain the artichoke hearts. Peel and slice the tomatoes. Mix together the avocados, artichokes, tomatoes, half the dressing and salt and pepper. Mix together the rice and remaining dressing and arrange on a serving dish. Pile the avocado mixture on top and garnish with the black olives. Chill before serving.

Hot Potato Salad
Serves 8

12 spring onions
45ml/3 tablespoons wine vinegar
1 kilo/2lbs small cooked new
    potatoes
25g/1oz chopped parsley
125ml/¼ pint oil
salt and pepper
125ml/5fl. oz natural yogurt
paprika pepper

Prepare the spring onions and chop finely. Heat the vinegar in a saucepan, add the potatoes, parsley, oil, salt and pepper and simmer for 3–4 minutes. Fold in the yogurt, turn into a serving dish and sprinkle with paprika.

The salad can be kept hot in the saucepan on the side of the grill.

Spanish Salad

Serves 8

1 lettuce
8 tomatoes
100g/4oz can anchovy fillets,
   drained
200g/8oz peeled prawns
16 Spanish stuffed olives, halved
125ml/¼ pint oil
60ml/4 tablespoons lemon juice
salt and pepper
1.25ml/¼ teaspoon dry mustard
1.25ml/¼ teaspoon sugar
4 hard-boiled eggs, sliced

Wash the lettuce, drain well, tear into pieces and place in a salad bowl. Peel, quarter and remove the seeds of the tomatoes, add to the lettuce with the anchovies, prawns and olives. Mix together in a screw top jar the oil, lemon juice, salt, pepper, mustard and sugar, cover and shake well. Pour over the salad and toss well. Decorate the salad with the sliced hard-boiled eggs.

Bean Sprout Salad

Serves 8

300g/12oz fresh bean sprouts
   (or 425g/15oz can)
100g/4oz onion, chopped
2.5ml/½ teaspoon dried tarragon
5ml/1 teaspoon dry mustard
10ml/2 teaspoons Demerara sugar
125ml/¼ pint oil
30ml/2 tablespoons wine vinegar
chopped parsley

Wash and dry the bean sprouts, put into a bowl and stir in the onion. Mix all the other ingredients together and pour over the bean sprouts; toss well and serve.

Spicy Rice Salad

Serves 8–12

200g/8oz long grain rice
2 tomatoes, chopped
1 red apple, cored and chopped
1 green pepper, de-seeded and
   chopped
285g/10oz can whole kernel
   sweetcorn, drained
100g/4oz button mushrooms, sliced
50g/2oz raisins
50g/2oz chopped walnuts
30ml/2 tablespoons French dressing
2.5ml/½ teaspoon ground nutmeg
salt and pepper
watercress

Cook the rice in boiling salted water for about 18 minutes, until just tender. Drain and rinse well under cold water. Put the rice in a bowl, add all the other ingredients, except watercress, and mix well together. Press the mixture into a 20cm/8in ring mould, chill for ½ hour in the refrigerator. Turn out on to a flat serving plate and fill the centre with watercress.
If no ring mould is available pile the mixture into a salad bowl.

Sour Rice Salad

Serves 8

200g/8oz long grain rice
250ml/10fl. oz natural yogurt
chopped parsley

Cook the rice in boiling salted water for about 18 minutes, drain well and put back in the saucepan. Add the yogurt and parsley and heat through. Do not over-heat as the mixture may curdle.

Chicory and Orange Salad

Serves 8

6 heads of chicory
2 oranges
45ml/3 tablespoons French dressing

Cut off the base and remove damaged outer leaves from the chicory. Cut into chunks, and wash and dry well with kitchen paper. Peel the oranges, removing all the pith and cut into thin rounds. Mix all the ingredients together and toss lightly.

Minted Cucumber and Celery Salad

Serves 8

1 medium sized cucumber
100g/4oz celery
10ml/2 teaspoons chopped mint
salt and pepper
juice of ½ lemon
125ml/5fl. oz soured cream
chopped parsley

Thinly slice the cucumber and chop the celery. Mix together all the ingredients and chill before serving.

Italian Salad

Serves 8

285g/10oz can cut asparagus
200g/8oz cooked diced carrots
200g/8oz cooked peas
8 stuffed olives
125ml/¼ pint Italian dressing
50g/2oz grated Parmesan cheese

Drain the asparagus, add all the other ingredients and toss lightly together. Chill well before serving.

Tomato and Fennel Salad

Serves 8

400g/1lb tomatoes
2 medium-sized roots of fennel
60ml/4 tablespoons oil
30ml/2 tablespoons wine vinegar
salt
ground black pepper
5ml/1 teaspoon sugar
2.5ml/½ teaspoon dry mustard

Wash and quarter the tomatoes. Wash the fennel and cut across the root into thin rings and mix with the tomatoes. Put all the other ingredients into a screw top jar, cover and shake well. Pour over the salad just before serving.

Piquant Endive Salad

Serves 8

2 heads of endive
1 bunch watercress
200g/8oz button mushrooms
salt and pepper
juice of 1 lemon
piquant dressing

Separate the endive leaves, wash well and dry. Wash and trim the watercress, toss the two together. Wash and thinly slice the mushrooms, sprinkle with lemon juice, salt and pepper and mix all the ingredients lightly together.

Vegetables

You can prepare most vegetables well in advance and then make full use of the barbecue by cooking them on the grill or wrapping them in foil and cooking directly in the coals. The vegetables can be kept very simple but a sauce or savoury topping can add extra flavour.

Barbecued Corn-on-the-Cob

To Choose Look for bright-green, snug husks (this shows the freshness) and the dark brown silk at the husk end – a sign of well-filled kernels.

To Store Cook fresh corn as soon as possible after buying or store in a refrigerator to preserve tenderness and sweet flavour.

To Cook – serve 1 corn cob per person.
a) Pull back the husks from the corn and remove the silk. Replace the husks and tie in place. Put the corn in boiling salted water for 3–4 minutes, then drain. Cook on the barbecue grill over hot coals for 12–15 minutes, turning frequently during cooking. Remove the husks and serve the corn with butter and salt.
b) After boiling the corn can be roasted in the coals for 10–12 minutes and then served as above.
c) Pull back the husks and remove the silk. Brush the corn with melted butter and sprinkle with salt and pepper. Pull the husks back over the corn again. Put each corn on a piece of foil, bring the sides of the foil together, twisting the ends to seal. Place the parcels on the grill and cook over hot coals for 20–30 minutes, turning each parcel once during cooking. If liked a crushed clove of garlic can be added to the melted butter before brushing on the corn.
d) Pull back the husks and remove the silk. Pour some barbecue sauce over the corn, pull back the husks and cook as above.

Saucy Onions
Serves 8

16 medium sized onions
salt and pepper
soy sauce

Peel the onions and put in pairs on to a square of heavy duty foil (or a double thickness of standard foil). Season with salt and pepper and a few drops of soy sauce. Screw the foil together to make a bundle and place it amongst the hot coals to cook for 30–35 minutes.

Potato Thins
Serves 8

8 large potatoes
2.5ml/½ teaspoon garlic salt
2.5ml/½ teaspoon celery salt
ground black pepper
30ml/2 tablespoons grated Parmesan
  cheese
200g/8oz butter

Peel the potatoes and cut into thin chips. Mix together the seasonings and cheese. Divide the potato chips on to 8 squares of foil, dot each with 25g/1oz butter and sprinkle with the seasoning. Bring the edges of the foil together to make a bundle. Allow plenty of room for expansion of steam in each bundle. Cook the bundles on the grill over medium coals for 25–30 minutes or until when tested with a skewer the potatoes are tender. Turn the bundles several times during cooking.

Courgette Boats
Serves 8

8 tomatoes
2 large onions
25g/1oz butter
salt and pepper
2 cloves garlic, crushed
2.5ml/½ teaspoon oregano
  oregano
8 large courgettes

Skin, seed and chop the tomatoes. Peel and chop the onions. Melt the butter in a frying pan, add the tomatoes and onions and fry for 4–5 minutes. Stir in the salt, pepper, garlic and oregano. Wash, top and tail the courgettes, and cut in half lengthwise. Sandwich two halves of courgette together again with some of the tomato mixture. Secure in two places with small pieces of cocktail stick. Wrap each courgette in a piece of foil and place on the grill. Cook over medium coals for 20–30 minutes.

Creamy Corn
Serves 8

75g/3oz cream cheese
425g/15oz can condensed celery
  soup
½ soup can of milk
2 285g/10oz cans whole kernel
  sweet corn
chopped parsley

In a saucepan mix together the cheese, soup and milk. Put the saucepan on the grill of the barbecue and heat over low coals until the cheese has melted. Add the sweet corn and heat for a further 5–6 minutes. Sprinkle with parsley before serving.

Spicy Whole Tomatoes
Serves 8

50g/2oz butter
50g/2oz onion, chopped
50g/2oz Demerara sugar
8 whole cloves
2 bay leaves
2 cinnamon sticks
5ml/1 teaspoon salt
ground black pepper
8 large tomatoes
125ml/¼ pint soured cream
chopped parsley
paprika pepper

Melt the butter in a small saucepan, add the onion and fry for 3–4 minutes. Add the sugar, cloves, bay leaves, cinnamon sticks, salt and pepper and cook a further 2–3 minutes. Wash the tomatoes and place each on a double thickness of foil. Lift the foil round the tomato to form a cup. Cut a cross in the top of each tomato and spoon over some onion mixture. Gather the foil at the top to make a bundle. Place the bundles on the edge of the coals and cook for 30–35 minutes. Carefully open the bundles and top each tomato with soured cream, chopped parsley and a dash of paprika pepper.

Stuffed Mushrooms
Serves 8

32 flat mushrooms
50g/2oz butter
1 large onion, chopped
25g/1oz grated cheese
50g/2oz streaky bacon, chopped
50g/2oz fresh white breadcrumbs
15ml/1 tablespoon chopped parsley
salt and pepper

Wipe the mushrooms, remove the stalks and chop the stalks finely. Melt the butter in a frying pan, add the mushroom stalks and onion and fry 3–4 minutes. Add all the other ingredients, except mushrooms, and mix well. Stuff the mushroom caps with the mixture and put the mushrooms on to squares of foil, four to a square. Screw the foil together to make a bundle and cook on the grill over hot coals for 15–20 minutes.

Jacket Potatoes
Serves 8

8 large potatoes
50g/2oz butter
salt

Scrub the potatoes, prick all over, rub with butter and sprinkle with salt. Place each potato on a square of double thickness foil. Bring the ends of the foil together in the centre and fold over two or three times. Turn the sides of the foil over twice and fold the ends underneath to make a sealed parcel. Push the parcels into the coals and cook for 50–60 minutes, turning once or twice during cooking. Pierce the foil with a fork to test that the potato is cooked. Open the parcel and cut a cross on the top of the potato; serve topped with butter, grated cheese, soured cream and chives or chopped parsley.

Broccoli Bundles

Serves 8

400g/1lb frozen broccoli
salt and pepper
2.5ml/½ teaspoon ground nutmeg
50g/2oz butter
30ml/2 tablespoons lemon juice

Place the broccoli on a square of heavy duty foil (or a double thickness of standard foil), season with salt, pepper and nutmeg and dot with butter. Sprinkle over the lemon juice. Bring the edges of the foil together and twist to form a loose bundle, leaving room for expansion of the steam. Cook on the grill over hot coals for 35–45 minutes, turning several times during cooking.

Asparagus spears can be cooked in the same way. Frozen peas can be used but add chopped mint instead of the nutmeg.

Golden Potatoes

Serves 8

50g/2oz butter
50g/2oz sugar
1 kilo/2lbs cooked small new
 potatoes
salt

Melt the butter in a frying pan on the grill of the barbecue, stir in the sugar and cook, stirring all the time, until the sugar has browned. Add the potatoes and toss them until a golden brown. Sprinkle with salt before serving.

Foiled Tomatoes

Serves 8

1 large onion
8 large firm tomatoes
cooking oil
salt and pepper
5ml/1 teaspoon oregano

Peel and cut the onion into 8 thin slices. Cut the tomatoes in half crosswise. Brush each half with oil and sprinkle with salt, pepper and a little oregano. Sandwich the tomato halves together again with a slice of onion in the middle and secure with a cocktail stick. Place each tomato on a square of foil, bring the corners of the foil together to form a bundle. Cook the bundles on the edge of the coals for 25–30 minutes until tender to the touch.

Buttered Aubergine

Serves 8

4 aubergines
150g/6oz butter
salt and pepper
ground nutmeg

Wash the aubergines and cut a thin slice from each end. Place each aubergine on a piece of heavy duty foil (or a double thickness of standard foil), dot with butter and screw the foil together to make a bundle. Bake in the coals for 45–50 minutes or until tender. Carefully open the bundles. Slice the aubergines and serve sprinkled with salt, pepper and nutmeg and the melted butter.

Fruit

A range of fruits are great fun to cook on the barbecue and what a delicious flavour they have; but no doubt you will want to serve a mouthwatering creamy concoction or a bowl of chilled fruit salad to round off a happy barbecue.

Bramble Syllabub

Serves 8

400g/1lb blackberries
30ml/2 tablespoons sugar
3 egg whites
150g/6oz caster sugar
finely grated rind and juice of 2
  lemons
125ml/$\frac{1}{4}$ pint dry white wine
250ml/$\frac{1}{2}$ pint double cream,
  whipped

Wash the fruit and put with the 30ml/2 tablespoons sugar into a saucepan, reserve 8 whole blackberries for decoration. Cook gently until the fruit is just soft. Allow to cool, then spoon the fruit into 8 tall glasses. Whisk the egg whites until stiff, then fold in the caster sugar, lemon rind and juice, wine and whipped cream. Pile the mixture into the glasses and top each with a whole berry.

Sugar Baby Party Bowl

Serves 8

$\frac{1}{2}$ Sugar Baby watermelon
caster sugar
60ml/3 tablespoons sherry

Remove the flesh from the melon and with a sharp knife cut a serrated edge around the shell to form a decorative bowl. Dice the flesh or form into balls with a melon ball cutter. Put into a bowl with the sugar and toss lightly until the sugar dissolves. Add the sherry and toss again. Pile into the Sugar Baby bowl and chill well before serving.
Cubes of other fresh fruit can be mixed with the watermelon to provide colour contrast.

Peach and Grape Tartlets

Serves 8

250g/10oz shortcrust pastry
250ml/½ pint double cream,
  whipped
820g/29oz can peach halves, drained
50g/2oz black grapes, quartered and
  pipped
45ml/3 tablespoons apricot jam
30ml/2 tablespoons brandy
10ml/2 teaspoons lemon juice
cinnamon

Roll out the pastry thinly and use to line 8 deep, fluted tartlet tins. Prick the bases with a fork and line each with a piece of foil. Bake in a moderate oven gas mark 6 or 200°C/400°F for about 15 minutes. Remove the foil and cook a further 2–3 minutes. Remove the pastry cases from the tins and leave to cool. When cold spread the bottom of each tartlet with a little whipped cream, place a peach half on top, and surround with the grapes. Heat together in a small saucepan the jam, brandy and lemon juice and brush thickly over the fruit. Leave to set. Put the remainder of the whipped cream in a bowl, sprinkle with cinnamon and serve separately.

Fruit Kebabs

orange segments
black and white grapes
pineapple pieces
apricot halves
banana
cherries
pear
apple

Brush the fruit with melted butter and cook on a grill over medium coals for 8–10 minutes, turning several times during cooking.
For a different flavour brush the fruit with a blend of melted butter, demerara sugar and ground cinnamon.

Grapefruit Mould

Serves 10

2 × 540g/19oz can grapefruit
  segments in natural juice
25g/1oz sugar
50g/2oz gelatine
375ml/¾ pint grapefruit juice
water
1 orange
1 eating apple
lemon juice
a few grapes

Drain the juice from the grapefruit segments. Put the juice in a saucepan, add the sugar and heat until dissolved. Remove the saucepan from the heat, cool a little then sprinkle on the gelatine and stir until dissolved. Add the 375ml/¾ pint grapefruit juice and make up to 1 litre/2 pints altogether with water. Cool until beginning to set, then stir in the grapefruit segments and pour into a wetted 1½ litre/ 2½ pint mould. Put in the refrigerator until set. Turn out on to a serving dish. Remove the peel and pith from the orange and cut into segments; core and slice the apple and sprinkle with lemon juice. Cut the grapes in half and remove the pips. Decorate the mould with the fresh fruit. Serve with natural yogurt or cream.

Gingered Pears

Serves 8

12 ripe pears
1 litre/1¾ pints water
200g/8oz sugar
75g/3oz preserved ginger, chopped
30ml/2 tablespoons ginger syrup

Peel, quarter and core the pears. Put the water and sugar in a saucepan and heat to dissolve the sugar. Add the pears, ginger and syrup. Cover and simmer for 5–10 minutes until the pears are just tender. Carefully turn into a serving dish and allow to cool. Serve with whipped cream, hazelnut yogurt or ice cream.

Spiced Apples

Serves 8

8 large cooking apples
200g/8oz mincemeat
100g/4oz butter
5ml/1 teaspoon ground cloves
125ml/5fl. oz natural yogurt

Wash and core the apples and make a slit round the centre of each to just score the skin. Place each apple on a square of double thickness foil. Fill the cavity with mincemeat, dot with butter and sprinkle with ground cloves. Wrap the foil round the apples to make a bundle. Cook on the grill over hot coals for 30–40 minutes. Serve the apples topped with yogurt.

Jamaican Grapefruit

Serves 8

4 grapefruit
60ml/4 tablespoons rum
60ml/4 tablespoons Demerara sugar
8 cherries

Cut the grapefruit in half, cut to loosen the segments and remove any pips. Place each half of grapefruit on a double thickness of foil, bring the edges up round the fruit and pour over the rum and sprinkle with sugar. Place a cherry in the centre of each fruit and twist the edges of the foil together to make a bundle. Put the bundles on the grill and heat over hot coals for 10–15 minutes.

Orange Cheesecake

Serves 8

12 digestive biscuits
25g/1oz cocoa
25g/1oz caster sugar
70g/2½oz butter, melted
400g/1lb cream cheese
100g/4oz icing sugar
285g/10½oz can mandarin oranges
125ml/¼ pint double cream
little orange rind, softened in boiling water

Crush the biscuits, add the cocoa and sugar. Stir in the melted butter and press into the bottom of a lined 20cm/8in sponge tin. Chill in the refrigerator. Beat together the cheese and icing sugar until smooth. Drain the juice from the mandarin oranges and beat 30ml/2 tablespoons of the juice into the cheese mixture. Whip the cream and stir into the mixture. Pour into the prepared biscuit base and chill until set. To serve: lift the cheesecake out of the tin and carefully remove the foil. Place the cake on a serving dish and decorate with the mandarin oranges round the sides and the orange rind on top.

Fun things

Sticky Fingers

Cut a slab of madeira cake into 2.5cm/1in cubes. Spear each on a fork or skewer and dip into heated blackberry jelly then into condensed milk and roll in desiccated coconut. Toast over very hot coals for a few minutes. Eat from the fork, but be careful, they are hot.

Apricot pieces

Place a maraschino cherry in the centre of a canned apricot half. Thread on a skewer, brush with a mixture of melted butter and cinnamon and grill over hot coals for a few minutes. Roll in coconut before serving.

Easy Grilled Bananas

Simply place the required number of bananas in their skins on the grill. Cook for about 8 minutes, turning several times; Open the skin and dribble with golden syrup, maple syrup or honey – delicious.

Topped Pineapple

Brush pineapple slices with melted butter and grill for a few minutes; mix together natural yogurt, brown sugar and toasted flaked almonds and spoon on to the pineapple.

Scrumptious Mallows

Thread pitted dates and marshmallows alternately on skewers and toast over hot coals for a few minutes.

Coffee Can Rolls

Put bread rolls in a large coffee can, cover, make a few holes in the lid and put the can on the grill; turn frequently until the rolls are hot.

Buttered Oranges

Cut oranges into thick slices, brush with melted butter, sprinkle with brown sugar and cinnamon and grill for a few minutes.

Skewered Apples

Peel, quarter and core the apples. Thread on to skewers, brush with melted butter and grill until brown. Serve sprinkled with brown sugar and nutmeg.

Toasted Marshmallows

Give each guest a long skewer and a pile of marshmallows. Impale a marshmallow on the skewer and hold close to the coals, twirling to completely toast the marshmallow. It can be dipped into melted chocolate or melba sauce before eating from the skewer.

Bread

Hot Savoury Bread

Cut a long French loaf diagonally into slices about 2.5cm/1in thick, but do not cut through the bottom crust. Spread the cut surfaces with one of the following:

> Cream 100g/4oz butter with 5ml/1 teaspoon each chopped parsley and chives; or
> 2.5ml/½ teaspoon curry powder; or
> 2 cloves garlic, crushed; or
> 2.5ml/½ teaspoon mixed herbs

Wrap the bread in foil and put on the grill or at the side of the coals to heat through, turning frequently, for about 10 minutes.

Pitta Bread

A flat oval bread from Greece. It makes a very convenient "pocket" or envelope in which to serve kebabs or burgers with a salad. It can be bought already cooked from Greek shops and is also available at Freezer shops. To use: just heat it in the oven or wrap in foil and heat on the grill of the barbecue. As it heats the bread puffs up, make a slit along the long side and there is the pocket to use.

Cheese and Onion Round

Serves 6–8

1 round stoneground loaf
75g/3oz butter
5ml/1 teaspoon made mustard
50g/2oz grated Parmesan cheese
50g/2oz onion, finely chopped
15ml/1 tablespoon chopped parsley
finely grated rind and juice of 1 lemon

Cut the bread into 1.25cm/½in slices. Mix together all the other ingredients and spread each slice of bread with the mixture. Put the loaf together again, cut in half through the centre and put on to a piece of foil. Gather the edges of the foil together to make a parcel and heat on the grill or at the side of the coals for about 20 minutes, turning frequently.

Savoury butters

Savoury Butter

100g/4oz softened butter mixed with one of the following:

5ml/1 teaspoon chilli powder
5ml/1 teaspoon curry powder
5ml/1 teaspoon oregano
5ml/1 teaspoon chopped chives
5ml/1 teaspoon chopped parsley
5ml/1 teaspoon chopped mint
2.5ml/½ teaspoon dill seed
5ml/1 teaspoon tarragon

Horseradish Cream Whip

Serve as a topping for steaks, ham or jacket potatoes

150g/6oz cream cheese
25g/1oz sugar
30ml/2 tablespoons horseradish
juice of ½ lemon
few drops Tabasco sauce
125ml/¼ pint double cream

Beat the cream cheese and sugar together; add the horseradish, lemon juice and Tabasco sauce. Whip the cream until just stiff and fold into the mixture; chill before serving.

Barbecue Spread

100g/4oz butter
2.5ml/½ teaspoon dry mustard
5ml/1 teaspoon salt
5ml/1 teaspoon paprika pepper
1 clove garlic, crushed
15ml/1 tablespoon sugar
finely grated rind and juice of 1 lemon
50g/2oz onion, finely chopped
30ml/2 tablespoons Worcestershire sauce
15ml/1 tablespoon tomato ketchup
few drops Tabasco sauce
30ml/2 tablespoons vinegar

Cream the butter until soft, then gradually beat in all the other ingredients. Store in a covered container in the refrigerator. Use to spread on steaks during grilling and just before serving. Do not use on very fatty meats.

COOKING CHART FOR GRILLING

Food	Cut	Weight/ Size	Fire Heat	COOKING TIME–EACH SIDE		
				Rare (mins)	Medium (mins)	Well-done (mins)
Beef	Steak	2.5cm/1in	Hot	5–6	7–8	10–15
	Steak	3.75cm/1½in	Hot	6–7	9–10	12–15
	Steak	5cm/2in	Med/hot	8–10	15–18	20–25
	[1]Flank	Whole	Hot	4–5		
	burger	2.5cm/1in	Med/hot	4–5	6–7	7–10
	Tenderloin	Whole	Med/hot	12–15	18–24	
Lamb	Chops	2cm/¾in	Medium	4–5	6–7	8–10
	Chops	2.5cm/1in	Medium	5–6	7–8	10–12
	Cutlets	1–2cm/½–¾in	Medium	4–5	6–7	8–10
	Breast	2.5cm/1in	Medium	4–5	6–7	8–10
	burgers	2.5cm/1in	Medium	5–6	7–8	8–12
Pork	Chops	2.5cm/1in	Medium			15–18
	Chops	3.75cm/1½in	Medium			19–22
	Spareribs	Whole	Low			35–45
	Spareribs	2.5cm/1in	Medium			10–12
	Belly strips	1.25cm/½in	Medium			10–12
Veal	Chops	2.5cm/1in	Medium			9–12
	Steak	2.5cm/1in	Medium			10–12
Poultry	Chicken	Portion	Medium			20–35
	Duck	Portion	Medium	7–9	10–11	20–30
Ham	Steak	2.5cm/1in	Low/med			12–18
	Steak	3.75cm/1½in	Low/med			15–22
Skewers[2]	Beef		Hot	4–5	6–8	10–12
	Lamb		Medium	6–7	7–8	9–10
	Pork		Medium			12–18
	Veal		Medium			12–15
	Fish		Medium			8–12
	Chicken		Medium			10–12

[1] Flank steak should only be served rare for tenderness.
[2] The skewers need to be turned frequently during cooking and the time given is for the complete cooking time of any skewer.

Sausages	Large		Med/hot	7–8
	Chipolata		Med/hot	4–6
Fish	Cutlet	2.5cm/1in	Medium	4–8
	Fillet	1.25cm/½in	Medium	4–6
	Whole	300–400g/12–16oz	Medium	10–15

COOKING CHART FOR SPIT ROASTING

Food	Cut	Weight	Heat	COOKING TIME 60°C/140°F Rare hours	75°C/160°F Medium hours	95°C/190°F Well-done hours
Beef	Rolled ribs	2½–3kg/5–6lb	Med/hot	2–2½	2½–3½	3½–4½
	Sirloin	2½–3kg/5–6lb	Med/hot	1½–2	2¼–2¾	3–3¾
	Tenderloin	1–1½kg/2–3lb	Hot	½–¾	1–1¼	1¼–1¾
Lamb	Leg	2–3kg/4–6lb	Medium	1¼–1½	1½–2	2–3
	Rolled Shoulder	1½–2½kg/3–5lb	Medium	1¼–1½	1½–2	2–3
Pork	Loin Boned and rolled	2–3kg/4–6lb	Medium			1¾–2¾
	Shoulder Boned and rolled	1½–2½kg/3–5lb	Medium			1¾–2¾
Poultry	Poussin	300–500g/12oz–1lb	Medium			¾–1
	Chicken	1–2kg/2–4lb	Medium			1½–1¾
	Duck	1½–2½kg/3–5lb	Medium			1¼–2
	Pheasant	1–1½kg/2–3lb	Medium			1–1½
	Turkey	2–3kg/5–6lb	Low/med			2–3